A Confederate Soldier's Eloquent War

The Complete Diary of Samuel Lowry

Enlistment, Battles, Hardship and Death

Yorkville to Columbia, Charleston to Kiawah to Manassas to Petersburg

Finally borne home by servant Henry Avery

Author – Samuel Lowry

Transcriber – Mrs. Sumter L Lowry

ANNOTATION BY MICKEY BECKHAM
AUTHOR OF *COLONIAL SPY* AND
A TIME REVISTED

Copyright © 2008 Mickey Beckham
All rights reserved.

ISBN: 1-4392-1124-8
ISBN-13: 9781439211243

Visit www.booksurge.com to order additional copies.

AUTHOR'S NOTES AND ACKNOWLEDGEMENTS

The following is a statement by Sumter L. Lowry, whose mother provided him with this important historical document. He, in turn, copied it for all his family to have.

> **"This is a copy of the original Diary written by hand by Samuel Cosmo (Catawba) Lowry which was passed down to me by my Mother, Willie M. Lowry, and is now in my possession. I desire to have a copy of this Diary in the hands of each family of the Lowry-Avery Clan. It is a marvelous document portraying the courage, faith and dedication of this young man to those things he loved in life, his Family, his Home and his Southland. He was killed at the Battle of the Crater, Petersburg, Virginia, July, 1864. He was nineteen years old.**
>
>
>
> **Sumter L. Lowry
> Chief, Lowry-Avery Clan"**
>
>

What follows is the actual diary of the very young man who fought in the American Civil War or the "War Between the States", as his uncles would have called it. I have added annotation and some very small editing, correcting some misspelled words for the reader, but not correcting all misspelled words. The most significant annotation is from Mrs. Sumter L. Lowry, "Willie" M. Lowry, adding beautiful, factual information. She transcribed the document from his written notes giving the family a most important piece of work. To Mrs. Lowry-thanks for her labors and thanks for her epilogue.

Samuel Cosmos "Catawba" Lowry was from Yorkville, the city now called York, in the most northern reaches of the state of South Carolina, close to the North Carolina line. Catawba Lowry and other men shared something that many people have never taken the time to discover; soldiers on both sides of the war were accomplished in their writing ability. Read letters and notes from men in that debilitating war. You will be surprised how well they wrote.

However, among all those, it is hard to believe that many could write as eloquently as Samuel Lowry. He was far ahead of those his age in intellectual capacity for the English language. He was given to flowery phrases but also mind wrenching observations of men dying. He suffered at news of the death of his mentor, General Micah Jenkins, the superintendent of the Kings Mountain Military Academy in York; he agonized greatly over the death of General Stonewall Jackson. He was wounded himself, recuperating to return to fight again. As a humanitarian, he wrote and worried about the servants he had with him during the war. He noted Horace's death from natural causes with family grief; he was pained at the sickness of Henry Avery, the young man who was with him at the Battle of the Crater, who brought his body home to his mother, a heroic act.

In his writings he referred to servants as "my boy." No one seriously interested in American history should be put off by this. Notice also he never called a servant a "slave." Notice that when he spoke of black men in his company, he spoke, not only with respect, but with certain admiration and concern for their health.

This was an awful time in American history. Catawba Lowry saw things that no teenage boy inviting manhood with emerging kind thoughts of young women, should witness as evidenced by his song "Maggie at My Side". This was the worst war of it's kind, surpassing the American Revolution in the south, not necessarily in brutality but the number of men killed. He spoke of thousands killed and wounded in a single engagement, the dying of these men particularly horrible, owing to faster repeating rifles, than at any time previously seen in our history.

The great sadness is that Samuel Lowry's children's children and their children are not here today. They died when he died, his seed forever lost. But he speaks still, it is recorded here, written in his style, with his eloquent soldier's pen.

Acknowledgements to Jeremy Smith for posing as Henry Avery for the cover. Jeremy is from Charlotte, NC and President of the student body of Clinton Junior College in Rock Hill, SC.

Thanks also to the re-enactors of the Confederate 6th Regiment for posing for the front cover. Re-enactors on the cover are Tommy Pappas, William Cloninger, Erik Marcusson, Joseph Marett and John Wilson. Gerald Goins of the 6th Regiment arranged the photo shoot and we are grateful to him for the photo of the long grey line on the cover, as well as Mike Short of the same Regiment for his assistance.

The photograph on the cover was made possible by long time friend and colleague Barry Grant of Grant Productions in Rock Hill, SC. Thanks to Barry for consistent advice and expertise, not only as a professional but as a fellow Revolutionary War re-enactor. Email to Barry at bgproductions@comporium.net.

Thanks to Jeannie Marion of the York County Museum and Historical Brattonsville who helped facilitate Civil War photos which are used throughout the diary and additionally came from Ashley Barron of the Museum.

Particular thanks to old friend, Hugh Harrington, of Milledgeville, Georgia for advice and consultation. Hugh himself has books written on the Civil War, reflecting happenings in and around Milledgeville.

Finally, thanks for the encouragement from relatives of Samuel "Catawba" Lowry in the production of this diary, especially Bo Lowry of York, Fred Faircloth, President of the Rock Hill Coca Cola Company in Rock Hill, and to my wife Elizabeth "Betty" Allen Beckham, who edited and typed the document.

One of those special remembrances occurred while compiling this diary; it was brought home by Samuel Lowry's writing. I and my family lived for years in Charleston, SC. In 1981-82 we lived at 37 Meeting Street, a mansion built before the American Revolution. It was the headquarters of General Beauregard, commander of Confederate troops and we thusly slept in Beauregard's bedroom, ate in his kitchen, studied in his great room. He suffered from a bad stomach, keeping a cow in the back yard for fresh milk to soothe his gastric pain. Did the General have acid reflux?

I imagined many early morning hours that he, like me, made his way down the enormous and winding staircase to his first floor, with many things on his mind as I had 20th century things on my mind. I have greater respect for him and his angst, having read Samuels' diary. I hope you enjoy this work and gain a particular insight as well. Mickey Beckham. Email to mickeybeckham@gmail.com

MEMORIUM

This book is in memory of three black men who accompanied Catawba Lowry during the war. They, Horace, Jesse and Henry, served as servants. They foraged for food, help procure it and prepare it; they walked miles and slept as they could with rain, cold and wind on them as warriors did in the Confederate army. They worried about their families, thought about being killed by shells and bullets, considered their uncertain fate if captured by Northern troops and longed to just go home accompanying their white family member.

One man, Henry Avery, bearing Catawba's maternal family name of Avery, brought Catawba Lowry's body home from Petersburg, Virginia after his death from the monstrous Battle of the Crater. In those days the body would have been wrapped in tar completely and placed in a coffin packed with field straw, then the coffin wrapped in tar again to keep the body decomposition smell from overwhelming those responsible for it. Oftentimes, when a body was transported, the smell would be so bad, the coffin would have to be dumped from a train by the railroad tracks.

It is logical that Henry Avery made his way by train eventually arriving in York. It was common that the train would have come from Chester, SC, a major depot. As it approached Yorkville, the train conductor would blow the train whistle to alert the populous that the train was arriving with news and dispatches. If it was good news the whistle would be blown in rapid bursts. If it was sad news or news of a major defeat in battle, the whistle blew long mournful sounds. On this day it blew long mournful sounds. The Lowry-Avery family may very well have gone to the depot to hear the news, then to their horror and surprise, receive the heart breaking news from Henry Avery.

DEDICATION

Samuel's writings are dedicated to his family of citizens, the Lowry-Avery clan, who are of English and Irish heritage marking their contributions in the beginning of the young colony of South Carolina before the American Revolution.

This book also recognizes two modern sons of York, SC in Charles Randolph Wright and John Spratt. Both men are nationally accomplished in their own way.

Charles Wright is a director, writer, and producer for theatre, television and film as well as a philanthropist. He is an honor graduate of Duke University, an A.B. Duke Scholar where he was a pre med student. He studied acting with the Royal Shakespeare Company in London and dance with the Alvin Ailey School in New York City. Among many credits his play, "Blue", starring Felisha Rashad, broke box office records at Arena Stage, the Roundabout theatre in New York. He directed the 50th anniversary tour of "Guys and Dolls" starring Maurice Hines. He has honored his family and his roots as a founding member of the Wright Family Foundation of South Carolina.

The Foundation has connected strongly with York, SC and the Rock Hill area by establishing the Alice Wright Smith Museum to preserve a family history of slavery from the time of a free black man to the present day. The Foundation is giving back to York and York County working with the York County Cultural Heritage Foundation to develop expertise in historical preservation.

Congressman John M. Spratt is a York native, graduate of York High School, who chose law and the political process as his life's work, incorporating into his career as a farmer, president of a bank and an elder in the Presbyterian church. He is a graduate of Davidson

College, Oxford University in England, and Yale University, the latter a degree in law.

He was a Captain in the US military before coming home. Most notably he is now Chairman of the Budget Committee, helping shape the federal budget. He is the second ranking Democrat on the Armed Services Committee and serves on three subcommittees, Oversight and Investigations, Strategic Forces and Air and Land Forces.

Both men represent York and South Carolina well; and both men carry with them the good fiber and character of men and women, their ancestors, in that period known as the American Civil War.

A CONFEDERATE SOLDIER'S ELOQUENT WAR

THE COMPLETE DIARY OF SAMUEL "CATAWBA" LOWRY;
ENLISTMENT TO HARDSHIP, BATTLES AND DEATH
YORKVILLE TO COLUMBIA TO CHARLESTON, TO KIAWAH,
TO MANASSAS TO PETERSBURG,
FINALLY BORNE HOME BY SERVANT HENRY AVERY

"I got a soldier to fill my canteen with water and I used that simple but most healing restorative, on my wound, just pouring it on the spot to keep the fever out of it. I finally got a Virginia doctor to bind up my leg and I felt very comfortable the rest of the night."
                                          Lieutenant Samuel Lowry

"THIS BEING OUR FIRST CAMPING GROUND..."

Samuel joined the Confederate army in November 1861, when the chill of first fall on honeysuckle, wild flowers alike, foretold frost, the coming winter, when cold ground replaced the heady summer days he enjoyed. It was appropriate that he joined in late fall when the dying of nature was apocryphal in his venerated Yorkville, the "Charleston of the upcountry." His enlistment was only a year from the time his uncle, William Blackburn Wilson, signed the ordinance of succession in Charleston, a historical note, breaking away from the United States. Lincoln had not yet been in office long before Samuel was aware that he had a new President, Jefferson Davis, a West Point graduate and former army officer.

Listening to his uncles, John Avery and William Wilson, he begged his parents to let him join the army. He solicited them with the news that Horace, a black man of the family would go with him, along with uncles and other cousins, making the service seem even more familiar.

Samuel Cosmos "Catawba" Lowery was sixteen years old, soon to be seventeen when his parents consented.
                                                    Mickey Beckham

"I will now proceed to give, as well as I can recollect from memory, the different incidents that occurred to myself and Regiment during my connection with the Southern Army, a period of 12 months. My Company left Yorkville on the 27th day of November, 1861 and proceeded from there by railroad to Camp of Instruction at Columbia, on the College Grounds. The Company to which I belonged was called The Carolina Rifles, commanded at that time by my Uncle, Capt. William B. Wilson, having for Lieutenants 1st Lieut. J. W. Avery, another Uncle of my own, 2nd Lieut. D. L. Logan, 2nd Lieut. R. H. Whisonant. Our company consisted of 100 men, from York District, all as stout and hardy a set of men as ever left the peaceful firesides of home to meet the foul oppressor. I was only entering lacking two months of my 17th year, having obtained the consent of my parents, after worrying them out begging them, and having two uncles in the company.

As I left off, we proceeded to the Camp College Green at Columbia, South Carolina, where we remained for a week drilling. I have been for two years a pupil at the Kings Mountain Military Academy, and being well drilled I was kept busily employed in assisting to drill the Company. This being our first camping ground, and being then something new, we had our fun, sitting around the camp fires, cracking jokes, and telling tales.

After staying here a week we moved out of Columbia to Camp Hampton, 5 miles distance, on the plantation of the now celebrated Brig. Gen. Wade Hampton. We encamped on an open old field formerly a race course. We pitched our tents amidst the rain, which was then pouring down in torrents, getting a thorough wetting, but we soon pitched our tents, and building some cheerful fires, we soon got dry and comfortable. While staying at this, one of our most pleasing Camps, I spent my time most agreeably, playing our camp games, living on boxes from home, filled with substantial food, such as meat and bread, which we ate with unusual appetites, cooked on our camp fires.

I may as well here name my mess mates and the faithful servants who attended us through all our hardships. My mess mates were the Captain and three Lieutenants, W. H. Moore and W. B. Byers, Capt. Wilson's servant, and the head cook was named Dick. Lieut. Avery's was named Noah, a stout built Mulatto, full of fun, and as faithful as the days long. My boy was called Horace. He was about 40 years of age, and one of the best and most faithful of negroes, who I afterwards had the lamentable misfortune to lose by a disease, concocted in camp. So you see, we were well waited on. These boys added a great deal to our amusement by telling their wonderful tales, and singing songs around the camp fires at night.

To return: The spot on which we were encamped was bordered on one side by large ponds, known as Hampton Ponds. In these ponds I sometime went duck hunting, finding plenty of the feathered tribe, but they were extremely wild. One day, having better luck than usual, I succeeded in killing two very large Dock O Mallards, over which we had a royal feast, prepared by the skillful hands of our cooks. My uncle and myself went out several times to hunt them, and sometimes with success. I fished some in these ponds, but it was too late in the year and consequently, I failed to catch any.

While at this camp we spent our time mostly drilling, and performing the various duties of camp. It was here also that our Regiment was organized, officers elected, etc. The following officers were elected: Ex-Governor John H. Means, Colonel, who afterwards proved his right to this and higher honors by his evident ability, by the valor he displayed, by the confidence of his Regiment, and at last by his glorious death on the heroic plains of Manassas. Fitz W. McMaster, Lieut. Colonel. Never was man better fitted for office than the heroic and chivalrous McMaster. I do not overrate his powers in thus describing him. Suffice it to say, time will prove. Julius Mills was elected Major; a man in every way worthy of the office, being an excellent officer and high toned gentlemen. Our Regiment thus organized, we now received orders to move to Charleston, which we did after a stay of two weeks at Camp Hampton.

Our route and next camp I will now describe. Having received our orders and a train of cars standing in readiness for us, we got aboard about six o'clock one morning, in box cars with plank seats, which, by the by was very good. We travelled over the well known track all day, until about one o'clock at night, being delayed by having to wait on other trains to pass us, the cars were very crowded and warm, we knocked off several side planks to admit the air, sometimes riding on top of the cars, which is very dangerous, but is not thought of. We arrived in Charleston about one o'clock at night, and landed at the depot, where a substantial supper of bread and coffee awaited us, of which I did not partake very heartily. After supper some of the men slept in the depot, others in the cars, I went back to the car and picking out the softest plank I could find, lay down, and was soon wrapt in the arms of Morpheus.

The next day we disembarked our baggage, shouldered our knapsacks, marched through the city and crossing the Ashley river by bridge, encamped immediately on the other side, that is on the right bank; this camp was christened Camp Lee. We remained here nearly a month, passing our time with the daily routine of camp duty, and occasional visits to the city. Sometimes I would hunt squirrels, of which I found plenty, but it being the proper season for fishing, and fishing in salt water being something new to me, I spent a great deal of my time fishing. My luck here hardly ever exceeded anything else than catching any amount of crabs, a sport I took great delight in at first, but of which I soon grew tired, especially as I could never bring myself to eat them or oysters, of which we had plenty, nor any other thing of the kind, although my two uncles gloried in them. I went out several times rowing in row boats on the river, and sometimes trying our skill in managing a boat with sails, run aground, and stuck fast until we hired some negroes to pull us out. But I soon learned to row a boat very well. It was at this camp that measles and mumps broke out among us, and for a time laid up nearly the whole Regiment, some dying from the effects of them. I fortunately had had the measles, but not the mumps. A great many were sent home on furlough to get well, and our Regiment was for a time thinly reduced.

It was about this time also that one of my cousins came down and joined the Company, and who was with us as long as I stayed, and is still a member. William Dunovant being about my age, we were nearly always together.

From this camp I went home on a short visit, and while I stayed at home the mumps, which I had several chances to catch, came out on me, though very slightly. I soon got perfectly well, and after staying at home about 3 weeks, I started back to Camp, but while I had been away the Regiment had been ordered away from Camp Lee and had moved to Johns Island and camped at a plantation on the Island, and named the camp Craft, from its owner. They stayed here only a few days and moved lower down on the Island to Camp Craft No. 2. Our company was sent out on picket to Rockville, but nothing as I understand of importance occurred. The Regiment afterwards moved to Curtis Plantation, and named this camp, one at which we remained a long time, Camp Fellow. It was here that I joined the Regiment, and came up with my company.

We were encamped here for about two months, and numerous little instances, marches, pickets, forages, etc. occurred here, which I will relate in turn as they occurred. Our camp was in an open old field, the largest I've seen on the Island, very level, and excellent for drilling. We spent our time in various ways, walking over the island, viewing the different beautiful residences and the unfragrant scenery of a lowland swamp, fishing in the creeks, hunting, playing ball, and hunting something to eat. The first two days or so we spent in fixing up our camp, making rude benches and tables, putting straw in our tents to sleep on.

After getting fixed up I began to wander about the Island, in the swamps, looking at the various kinds of vegetation on the lookout for some animal worth shooting with my pistol which I generally carried with me, and hunting for magnolias and such things as I knew would be prized at home, some of which I sent home. I went about to several of the nearest houses, deserted by their owners on account of the Yankee's proximity. In several of these houses there was a great deal of furniture, some of it costly, such as beds, bureaus, sofas and sometimes pianos, &c. of which a great deal had been destroyed by some ruthless hand, a great many old books and such things as was needed in camp, when we found them we did not scruple to take. We spent a great deal of our time in camp making little rings out of cow and deer horn and beef bones, some of these were very beautiful, and of superior workmanship. I went out several times on little fishing excursions with my uncle Avery, but generally failed to catch anything else but crabs and eels, but I saw some negroes that understood the art bringing up buckets full of fish & crabs and shrimps.

I took great interest in going out in little boats with these boys and watching them fishing. We lived mostly on sweet potatoes, of which any quantity could be found, of superior quality. I went out with the wagons several times after them, getting the wagons loaded and then looking about the garden and premises for something further in the eating line, such as a stray sheep, and very often we went out cow hunting, that is, some of us would be sent out on the Island to kill beeves for the Regiment, plenty of which were to be found stray and almost wild on the Island.

One day W. Dunovant, myself and several others were sent out to kill them. We went about 4 miles from camp over on Wadmalaw Island. We soon came across a small drove, and encircling them fired into them, each one of us dropping one. Then came the work skinning them. I assure you it is no fun for we tugged and worked for an hour or so, but we soon got used to such work, and was generally glad to get a chance to skin them, in anticipation of a good meal. Very often we were sent out foraging on the different plantations and islands around us, sometimes bringing fodder and hay for the horses, sometimes potatoes for ourselves. I was always very glad to go on these expeditions, as I got a view of the country, and generally got something extra to eat for my own mess, such as a sheep, duck, &c, besides these, in some a manner pleasant employment.

We very often had to go on expeditions just the contrary. After we had stayed on the island a short time, we were put to work building a road across the marsh and then a bridge over the Stone River, at Church Flats, to the mainland, A detail of men from each company was sent every day to work on them. Our times came 'round quite often, and we would either have to cut wood or brush or dig up dirt, or some other hard labor; this was very tedious and a very dirty work. We were continually in the mud, and on some of these expeditions we would sometimes come across a bee hive, or a stray sheep, or some other thing. One day I got a large Muscovy Duck which represented as being wild.

As these were our every day employments, we had our fun at night, when not on guard. We had an over plus of fiddlers in the Regiment and every night a ring was soon formed and a nimble negro in the middle, we had dancing, far superior to the cramped steps of a fashionable hall. But when the guard turn comes, then our amusement stops for awhile, and the stern duty of a soldier, tramping his lonely path, thinking of the dear ones at home, usurps for awhile the jovial mood.

As he walks along his lonely post, liable at any moment to be ushered into the presence of an offended God, by the hand of an unseen foe, listening to the mad howl of the wolf, the hoarse croak of the frog and the shrill cry of the never tiring whippoorwill, his comrades wrapt in a slumber so coveted by him. 'Tis then he thinks of war, and its horrors, of duty and its rewards, of disgrace and its consequences. Then the loved forms of dear ones at home flits across his mind; he views them in his imagination, sitting before the glowing fire of a peaceful home, talking of him so long absent, and then it is that sweet recollections of the past present themselves, to sooth as it were, his troubled feelings. But hark: the fierce cry of the sentinel's halt again awakens him to a sense of duty, and such duty as a struggling country demands of her sons, fighting the battles of freedom."

"WE MARCHED ON THROUGH THE BEAUTIFUL VILLAGE..."

> Samuel would soon be camping and sleeping, looking for war, in what is today a paradise of lush greens and foliage on the resort of Kiawah Island. The bounty of fish, crabs, oysters, all seafood on the barrier islands is still coveted and eaten with much delight as when he, Horace and others, Yankees and Confederates, foraged for them. In the 21st century the tranquility bought and paid for by young men who clamored over the dunes, then marveled at the beauty of the islands is forgotten. In our time it is taken for granted, but paid for, nevertheless, with a price later on at Gettysburg, Manassas and Petersburg and many other places.
>
> Mickey Beckham

"But to return. I will now notice our first picket, and give facts as near as I remember. Our Company was ordered by the Colonel to go on picket to Rockville on outskirts of Wadmalaw Island in perfect site of the enemy's gunboats about a half mile distance in the Edisto River, and in sight of their camp fires on Edisto Island. Accordingly we left Camp provided with a week's rations, a blanket strapped to each ones back, and shouldering our muskets, struck the march for Rockville, 15 miles distance. We marched by fours, and about three in the evening reached a house two miles from Rockville, and took up quarters for the company in the house, pretty weary and tired. The first night was not mine to stand guard, which was very fortunate for me as I was somewhat fatigued.

We slept soundly that night, and rising next morning, felt considerably refreshed. Clubbing together we formed little parties, going about on the Island, some in search of something to eat, some for simple curiosity, and others for books and camp plunder, &c. The coming night was the night for picket, and the company fell in and marched down to Rockville, marching along behind the hedges and fences to keep out of sight of the Yankee lookouts, to whom we did not wish our whereabouts to be known. Just as we got in the vicinity of Rockville a very heavy rain shower came up, drenching us to the skin. We marched on through the beautiful little village, one of the prettiest that I have ever seen, and we took up quarters in one of the largest houses, and after stationing pickets on the banks of the river to watch for boats, we lay down on the floor and was soon sound asleep.

Nothing of importance occurred that night. The next night was my turn for picket, and when it arrived my Captain took me down to the river banks, stationed me there, and ordered me to watch for boats, and if I saw any, to fire on it, and retreat to the house. I took my post, with a blanket around me to keep off the shrill, cold sea wind, and I stood and watched the rolling expanse of waters before me until I was tired out.

About midnight I got so sleepy that I could hardly keep my eyes open, and every now and then would drop off in a gentle snooze, and would be awakened by the loud blowing of the porpoise in the river, or the constant dash of the waves on the shore. I thought it the longest night ever human mortal experienced, and I fervently wished a boat with Yankees would come along, that I might fire into her, but none came. The Captain brought me a chair about midnight; I sat down in it, trying my best to keep awake until morning, but would occasionally drop off into little snoozes. But, joy divine, I at last saw the bright light of day begin to dawn, and night's dark mantle was withdrawn.

Then I was relieved after standing post the whole night, from dark until daylight, then leaving a picket in the place, we marched the company back to our temporary quarters. When I got back to the house the first thing I did was as Dick, the cook, said, to eat a pound and a half of bacon, with bread in proportion, and then for sleep, but strange to say, I could not sleep, but was running about all day with the boys, sometime sailing on the tide in a leaky boat, and again catching crabs and gathering oysters. That evening Lieut. Logan came down to us, who had been home on sick furlough, and brought us orders to repair to camps instantly as the Regiment had received marching orders.

Accordingly, we withdrew the pickets and took up line of march for camps. I was no little fatigued in this march, but kept up as well as any, as I always made it a point never to break down as long as one leg would follow the other, but I had stood guard the preceding night, not sleeping of any consequence, for 48 hours, and was necessarily tired. When we got to camp all was quiet as ever, the marching orders having been countermanded. So we were once more back into our old camps, and I tell you what, I did some tall sleeping that night. The next morning I got up considerably refreshed, and for several days we lolled about the camps, playing ball, fishing, drilling &c.

One day I went up to one of the large swamps, close by us, taking my gun, and killed a small alligator, of which there was a great plenty, but could not get him out of the water. Also, there were a great many cranes all 'round us, and finding some of their nests, I climbed up to them and got the eggs, over which I had a superb feast when I got back to camp. My faithful old servant Horace attended me in these marches, ever careful to procure my comfort as he best could, carrying me little extra bites of some thing to eat, always having my dinner, and cooked at the proper time. We did not have very many expeditions while at this camp, besides two or three other trips to Rockville, Bears Bluff, and of little consequence, and several forages and false alarms, caused sometimes by the sentinels firing at imaginary enemies, or discharging their guns by accident or carelessness.

I went on several forages. I went on a forage once on Kiawah Island, right on the sea coast with A. McElwee and the Major and Commissary Captain, W. B. Metts, of the Regiment. I rode in a little wagon with the former mentioned gentleman. The distance was about 25 miles. We passed on to Seabrooks plantation, where a few days before the Stone Scouts had a brisk skirmish with the Yankees, the marks of the combat were distinctly to be seen on the trees and surrounding houses, which were perforated with balls. Here we crossed river by bridge over on Seabrooks Island, we struck across the island and soon arrived at the other side, and crossed another stream on a very dilapidated bridge, over to Kiawah Island. From here we had a distinct view of the sand hills on the ocean beach. As we got on the Island we struck on to a little road, just wide enough for the wagons to pass through, with a jungle on each side of palmettos and other low country vegetation so thick that you cannot see five steps into it, to let alone penetrating it.

We proceeded, and at length arrived at one of the plantations at the extreme verge of the island, where we found several negroes, the only persons on the island, from whom we bought all the chickens and eggs they had, and several young lambs, with which we loaded our wagons. Then Capt. Metts lending me his horse, I with the rest of the party, two excepted, rode down to the beach to see the ocean. Accordingly we rode down there and rode along the beach for three miles or so, occasionally dismounting to pick up some pretty shell, any quantity of which were scattered around us. I filled my pockets, it being in some respects new to me.

We rode on until our guide, Capt. Walpole, discovered a footprint freshly made in the sand, and knowing it to be one of our enemies, with the true instinct of a scout, grew cautious, and we turned into a little path and rode on until we reached the main road conducted by our guide, without whom we would have been certain to have gotten lost. We soon caught up with the wagon and proceeded to camp without accident, arriving about nine at night when, after unloading the wagon, we retired to our tents and arose next morning considerably refreshed in mind and body.

We remained on Johns Island some 3 weeks, making our stay about two months in this camp. Nothing of any consequence occurring except the reorganization, in which the Regiment enlisted for the war, all over 35 years of age and under 18 being exempt after 90 days after 72 months. This caused a decided change in the Regiment. Some new officers were elected and others retiring home being exempt. R. S. Means was elected Major, vice, Major Mills. The Colonel and Lieut. Colonel were reelected. Capt. Wilson, being exempt by his age, went home, though greatly against the wish of the company, to which he had endeared himself by many kind acts. Our 1st Lieut. J. W. Avery was elected Captain by the unanimous vote of the company. Lieut. Logan was elected 1st Lieutenant and our 3rd Lieut. also leaving us, R. H. Whisonant. Two vacancies were left, 2nd Lieutenant and Brevet 2nd, to which places E. T. Moore and W. Moore were respectfully elected. So we had an entire reorganization and it was the same in most of the companies of the Regiment."

"NEXT MORNING MY SHOES WERE FILLED WITH WATER THRU AND THRU…"

> *So, Samuel lost his uncle, William Blackburn Wilson, not to war, but to his uncle's age. With some little serendipity, but mainly rules of that day, men left camp, without war, to live another day, some to live until the 1900's. Samuel learned–his character forged without his being totally aware of it–not to sleep on duty, go 48 hours without sleep if necessary, but remain faithful. His battle character had its genesis on these islands; it would serve him well in the mud pits of a siege far to the north at another time.*
>
> Mickey Beckham

"I will now speak for myself. Being under 18, I could not get the consent of my parents to enlist for the war, so my turn was 12 months and 90 days, having then some 8 months service before me. I forgot to state that it was here that my old Servant, Horace, took sick, and getting worse I sent him home, where the poor fellow died about two weeks after this. My father and brother, also my cousin Leon Massey paid us a visit, bringing to me another servant called Jesse, a likely young fellow of about twenty, who afterwards stuck to me thru thick and thin, and of whom I never had cause to complain.

We remained on the Island a good while afterwards, lying still in camp, living on low bush black berries, any quantity of which were all around us, and of which we had delicious pies prepared by our skilful cooks. Then receiving marching orders we took up line of march and crossing the causeway and bridge that we had completed at Church Flats after a very hot and dusty march of 15 miles, encamped at Rantoules Station on the Charleston and Savannah railroad, a very pleasant place. This we named Camp Simons No. 1, here pitching our tents we soon rested from our hot and fatiguing march. We had only remained in this camp a short time, employing our time fishing and drilling, when we were summoned back to Church Flats to oppose a gunboat or two that was said to be advancing up the river which proved to be one of those common false alarms, to which we were always subject and which were constantly occurring. However, were detained here for several days without tents, but crowded in little huts so close that we hardly had room to turn around. I generally prefer the open air if not raining and slept out of doors.

One night my cousin and myself spread our blankets under a large oak, and were soon sound asleep. About midnight a very heavy rain storm came up and pattering rain in our faces we were soon awakened. My cousin, arising after it began to come down pretty hard, ran into the house, but I, with singular foolishness, drew blankets and oil cloth over my head and sat there, taking the rain which poured down in irresistible torrents. In a minute, it began to run under me, then I jumped up in my stocking feet and ran through the muddy water to the house, leaving shoes which, for a wonder, I had pulled off, and gun, and accoutrements. Next morning my shoes were full of water, and I had some difficulty in drying them. My guns and accoutrements were not hurt. I spent about as much of my time while here in the river bathing, where I first learned to swim.

After staying here two or three days we returned to camp, seven miles distance, where we arrived in a short time. We made one or two other marches from the camp only about two weeks, from where the camp was removed from this place lower down on the railroad, to the little village of Ravenel, about 10 miles distance, in a very healthy and pleasant situation, right by the side of the railroad. This camp was named Camp Simon No. 2, where we remained until our removal to Virginia. But from this camp we took on several hard marches and expeditions, which I will relate in time.

The first expedition was to Pocotaligo, from there to Port Royal Ferry. We were lying quietly in camp with nothing to do but sleep, eat, drill and run about the country, when a courier came dashing up to the headquarters bringing information of the Yankees landing at Port Royal Ferry and marching towards Pocotaligo, to cut the railroads, said to be several thousand strong, with orders for us to repair immediately to Pocotaligo to resist the advance. I happened to be on guard at the time in camp and was in a state of mental excitement, bordering on to madness for fear I would be left in camp and would not get to go, but I soon get a substitute to stand guard in my place and let me go. Pocotaligo was 50 miles distance, but a train of cars soon being ready for us we went like the wind and soon arrived there about sunset in the evening. As we landed the cavalry pickets came up saying the enemy were retreating, after being driven back by our small body of cavalry in a spirited skirmish, with some loss on both sides and several Yankee prisoners.

Nevertheless, we immediately started in pursuit. The enemy had been within a mile of Pocotaligo when they retreated. We marched very fast without stopping to rest once until about ten at night and had marched some ten or twelve miles without seeing the enemy. Taking up line of march again after a short rest, we went some three miles further, when seeing no hope of overtaking the enemy we were ordered to halt and stop for the night in a large mansion. But our imaginations were not to stop here. Our company and Capt. Culps of our regiment were ordered to proceed to a bridge with a detachment of the Beaufort Artillery; also to defend the bridge, and if possible to intercept the march of the enemy, and defend our rear from a night attack.

Accordingly, feeling the full force of the old proverb, there is no rest for the weary, we again started for the bridge, said to be 3 miles distance, but we, by the route we went, soon found it out to be nearer 6 than 3 miles. We marched along in silence, not allowed to speak aloud, suffering greatly from want of water. Nothing was to be heard but our own dull, heavy tramp, the command of our officers, the hoot of the owl, the cry of the whippoorwill, and the black darkness of the night, all conspired to affect each one of us with thrilling interest, every moment expecting to see a body of Yankees oppose us, but none appeared. It may be as well to state here the whole detachment was under the command of Capt. Avery of my company and to no one could the trust have been better given. He was in every way qualified to carry out the enterprise, as he is to carry out any that can be given to him. He was nobly aided by the other officers also. We advanced very cautiously, constantly keeping an advance guard in front and rear guard behind. Just at this time an incident occurred which served to increase the interest of us all. Capt. Avery caught a horse standing in the middle of the road, rider less, but with saddle, bridle and sword of the owner buckled to him. We did not know what to make of it. Was it the horse of an enemy, who by our close pursuit had been compelled to abandon it, and if so, were not more about, and such like idle surmises, but the mystery was cleared up the following day as I will show you in time.

We grew more cautious after this, but marched on until at last we arrived at the bridge over a small river about two o'clock at night, fatigued, sleepy and hungry. Here upon the edge of the marsh we halted and, after stationing guards on the bridge and in our rear, tumbled down on our arms and were soon sound asleep with one blanket over us. When we arose in the morning we were wet with dew, but, building fires we soon got dry and the searching our haversacks for something to eat, which we found very scarce, and as the day were soon out entirely.

About nine o'clock in the morning we took up line of march and crossed the bridge, intending to form a junction with the regiment at the cross roads. We pursued our route and arrived at the cross roads and there we found a key to the mystery of the horse. On the side of the road, in a little ditch, lay the dead body of Dr. Godard a member of the Rutledge mounted riflemen, shot thru and thru by the enemy who had waylaid him and shot him from the bushes by the wayside and that was his horse that we had caught. Here we joined the regiment and fell into our place and pushed on to Fort Royal in pursuit, which was five miles distance, but were too late.

We arrived at the ferry just in time to give the enemy a parting salute without cannon causing them to scamper out of the way in double quick time. The enemy was driven back but no fight of any consequence had taken place. We were woefully fatigued, hungry and sore, but it would not do for us to stay there, and we were ordered to return.

We commenced the march about ten o'clock in the morning and hour after hour we trod along the sandy road under a burning sun, with sore feet and mouths dry with thirst. Sometimes I pulled off my shoes, and took it barefoot, but the hot sand compelled me to put them on again. We still persevered, some broke down, but at length the long looked for railroad came into sight. I have often thought this one of the hardest marches I ever took, being about 48 miles, with hardly any rest, under a burning sun. At Pocotaligo a train of cars carried us back to camp Simons where we soon rested from all our toils."

"WE STILL SUPPOSED A LARGE YANKEE INFANTRY IN FRONT OF US..."

> Samuel had seen death for the first time. It was only one man, to be measured small and horrible comparing the next months, one man's body murdered, left by the road. It would become usual to him to what he would see, hear, and write about. Loss of life would be measured not in the hundreds in weeks and months to come, but in the thousands. He would find that he would be able to reconcile better a man's death, than a man's dying, but it sharpened his senses to write. Had it not, he would have become a mental casualty himself. Of necessity, he steeled himself.
>
> Mickey Beckham

"We remained in camp about two weeks before we took up another march, and this march was back to Johns Island. A courier came dashing into camp suddenly, bringing news that the enemy had landed in strong force on Johns Island, and that the gunboats were advancing up the Stone River. The long roll was sounded, 3 days rations were gotten ready, and in an hours time we were on the march. We soon arrived at Church Flats on the Stone, and took up quarters on the banks of the river, while Col. Dunovant's Regiment of Regulars was sent over on the Island to oppose the advance and to serve as a vanguard for us. We remained at Church Flats until about four in the evening, when a Courier came up at full speed saying that the enemy was still advancing and that Donovant's whole Regiment had been cut off by the Yankees and were all prisoners. This caused great excitement. Everything was gotten ready, not doubting that we would have a tough struggle.

Orders were given and we took up line of march for the Yankees. We marched on until about 10 at night. The enemy was said to be in two miles of us. We were certain of having a hot fight on the morning, but slept soundly after the fatigue of the march. In the morning we marched down to the forks of the road where the Yankees were supposed to be, but we were mistaken. They were still further off. When we arrived at the cross roads, we received orders to halt and await the arrival and orders of Brig. Gen. Evans, commanding the whole force. I think he was rather tardy in all his proceedings, and through whose mismanagement a splendid opportunity was lost. For if he had have been with us that morning, we could have advanced against the enemy and no doubt have driven them off the island with loss, but they soon began to fall back again. When Gen. Evans arrived, the enemy had retreated into the neighborhood of Seabrooks Island.

On the arrival of Gen. Evans we were ordered to retire to a house a short distance back and spend the night, leaving a picket at the cross roads. Nothing of importance occurred that night; this was the second night on the Island. The following day we spent lolling about our temporary quarters, listening to the various reports brought in from the picket lines in front by our cavalry. About 4 p.m. a heavy thunder storm came on. The clouds were perfectly black, and seemed to be a forerunner of the bad mistake which occurred that evening. It had been raining all the previous night. The roads were very wet, but every now and then reports would again reach us that the enemy was advancing. About this time our pickets stationed at the cross roads sent in a man saying that a body of Yankees, both infantry and cavalry, were upon them and that they were in great danger of being cut off and for us to hasten to their relief. In five minutes we were ready and on the way to the picket lines two miles distance. Our picket numbered about 30 men, all cavalry.

We had gotten in about half mile of the line when a sad calamity, or rather, mistake, befell us. Just as we turned an angle in the road what was our surprise on seeing a body of horsemen immediately in front of us, at about ten paces, going, or rather, coming, at horse neck speed towards us. We had barely time to part to the sides of the road to save ourselves from being run over by these flying horsemen. We supposed them to be Yankees, but as the foremost neared us we saw them to be our pickets. The foremost man as he approached shouted out, "The enemy are right behind us," but it so happened that our men had divided into two squads on account of some horses being faster than others, and we took the first squad to be our pickets and the hindermost ones to be the enemy in pursuit, for all of them were going so fast no distinction could be made, and we were very naturally mistaken as the last squad, which we took to be Yankees, came up our first; two companies fired into them dropping men, horses, &c. in our confused melee.

Rain was pouring down and we were soaking wet, and the fact of a great many guns not firing saved several lives. It was bad enough. The cavalry likewise mistook us for the enemy and fired their pistols at us as they passed. Two Lieuts. in the Regiment and one private was wounded. I was standing right by one of the Lieuts. when he received his wound which was slight. I had just fired at the cavalry as they passed and was reloading when I heard the command given to form line of battle on the other side of the road. I immediately rammed home my bullet and ran across the road jumping over the dead and wounded lying in the road and took my place in line. The Yankees on hearing our fire immediately stopped their pursuit, wheeled, fired into us and left as fast as possible.

But we still supposed that a large body of Yankee infantry was in front of us and we immediately deployed on one side of the road. Forming line of battle we advanced, wading through the marsh sometime up to our hips, getting a thorough wetting. In the meantime torrents of rain poured down in all its fury, and such thunders as I never before heard. However, after reloading we kept steadily forward in line of battle. Having thrown out Capt. Hill's company as skirmishes in our front, all of a sudden the skirmishes fired into what they supposed to be a company of Yankee Infantry who immediately skedaddled. Proving to be cavalry, leaving one horse killed. The night was very dark and with difficulty we could see our hands before faces. Nothing more of the enemy was seen and we returned to learn of our unfortunate mistake in firing into our own men, but which was to be blamed entirely on our cavalry pickets. We had only returned a short time and were drying our clothes before large fires when our company was ordered out on picket to repair to the cross roads and remain as guard for the rest of the night.

We immediately left, and arriving at the cross roads pickets were stationed, and the utmost silence maintain. I was placed at one of the stations with two others, and remained standing the rest of the night, shivering with cold, but the bright Goddess of morn at length succeeded in raising the dark mantle of night and ushered in a bright sunny day. We were now relieved by Capt. John M. Witherspoon's company and returned to quarters to rest and eat and lay about all day, nothing occurring to excite interest. At dusk the regiment was again formed and marched down to the cross roads, but at dark Gen. Evans arrived and ordered us to leave the Island, and our whole force, excepting the cavalry, left, consisting of Dunovant's Regulars, 16th regiment and ours, the 17th. We got to Church Flats at about nine at night, tired and sleepy, having stayed on the Island a week.

The following day we repaired to Camp Simons for a short rest, for it was not long before we were again on the march. Our route and also our purpose this time was different from that which we hitherto pursued and something more exciting, for we had hitherto acted only on the defensive, but now we assured an offensive position. Attack was planned on the enemy on Edisto Island to be led by Col. Stevens of the Halcombe Legion, an able and excellent officer. We soon received orders, and with little preparation were on the march. First we went to Adams Run, the headquarters of Gen. Evans, about 12 miles distance from our camp. Here we met up with one or two other Regiments bound on the same expedition.

In truth our force was very small, being only the Halcome Legion, 17th Regiment, Nelson's Battalion, and some other separate commands of artillery and cavalry. a small force to undertake to drive ten thousand Yankees off of an Island so well fortified and defended. When we arrived at Adams Run we halted and spent the night out in the street.

The next day, by daylight, we were on the march for Edisto. We walked all day under a scorching sun, suffering from thirst and fatigue. We at length arrived at Pineburg the place of crossing over to Ichossee Island, at about sunset, having only one large flat to cross the whole body; we were a long time getting over. Our Regiment did not get over until about nine at night, when we took a small embankment for a path, thrown up just between the rice dams and the river, only a yard wide, with very tall grass growing on each side of it. It needed only one misstep on either side to precipitate us into the river on one side or the rice dam on the other, but luckily for us the moon was shining brightly. We kept up this narrow path for about three miles, following the course of the river until at length we reached a road leading to Ex-Gov. Aiken's plantation, and following it, soon reached his wealthy farm. It ought to be called a village as I never saw so great a number of negro houses together to be owned by one man and on the whole so well fixed. We stopped here to rest; it was then about 12 o'clock at night. We had hardly gotten seated on the ground when a courier came dashing through our ranks at headlong speed saying that the enemy was endeavoring to cut us off with their gunboats by sailing up the river, and were prepared to receive us on the Island, having been informed by some treacherous negro of our intentions, and as only half of our forces were yet over on (—here the writing is illegible—) orders were given for us to retreat.

We immediately marched back, leaving a picket behind. Taking the same route by the narrow path, we proceeded very slow and did not reach the ferry until about two o'clock. We were then compelled to stand in this narrow path for three hours and a half before we could cross, the tide having fallen and were compelled to wade thigh deep in mud and water before we could reach the flats. But we got over safe at last just as the gray tent of morn began to appear on the Eastern Horizon.

Having walked the whole night and the day previous we were pretty well wearied, and took a great rest at Pinebert, and about ten a.m. started for camp which we reached the following day, our march being all for nothing as it turned out to be. This was the last march of any consequence that we took on the coast. True, we made another trip to Pocotaligo once in the case of an alarm, but it proved to be false, and we returned. Our next experience now came to possess more the appearance of stern reality, and instead of false alarms we came to sturdy blows, and close contest with a powerful enemy. We received orders to repair to the Old Dominion, the land of fights, and were soon on the way."

"WE WERE ONE WEEK ON THE ROAD AND AT LAST WE REACHED RICHMOND....."

> Samuel and his comrades thought Virginia to be the "holy ground" where war would be fought to a successful conclusion. Robert E. Lee had assumed command from General Joseph E. Johnson when General McClellan of the North openly disdained Lee as a man likely to be timid and irresolute in action. From June 25 to July 1, Lee attacks McClellan near Richmond and McClellan withdraws back toward Washington. Then again 75,000 Northern troops under General Pope are defeated by 55,000 gray clad soldiers under Stonewall Jackson and James Longstreet; they also pull back toward Washington.
>
> Samuel is more than convinced the south will win. He longs for even more action. He calls Longstreet's corps "invincible."
>
> Mickey Beckham

"We were lying in camp at Camp Simons No. 2 when we received orders to get ready to leave for Virginia. A soldier's baggage, like his money, is always scarce, and we were not long in packing. All extra baggage was discarded, and boxes, baskets, tin pans, &c. were left strewn over the camp grounds. A train of cars soon came for us, and one car only being allowed to a company, we were necessarily crowded and warm, it being the last of June.

We got to Charleston about four in the evening, and were compelled to remain there until nine at night, for want of means of transportation to carry us. We were here greatly disappointed, and the whole regiment very angry. We had all entertained the idea of getting to go the upper road which could have taken us all close to home and was as near as any other way to Virginia, but when we got to Charleston it was decided to send us on the Wilmington and Manchester railroad, and I can tell you there was some tall cursing done that day, but it is a soldier's duty to obey orders and we were compelled to go the way we were ordered. We took our spite out in eating watermelons, and fruit, and a goodly number of them went down that well worn path, a Soldier's threat; we left Charleston that night at nine o'clock, and was fast carried away from the state of our pride and birth, some never to return again.

We passed through Old Rip by way of Wilmington and Goldsboro up to Welden, from thence to Petersburg and Richmond. We were one week on the road and at last we reached Richmond without the occurrence of anything worth mentioning. It was near ten o'clock at night when we reached Richmond. We were formed into lines in the streets and marched directly through them, saluted by deafening cheers by the populace, and the ladies looked timidly from their windows, and waved handkerchiefs and night-caps in abundance. We marched without tents, although raining a little, but we soon got to abhor tents, and would take the open air from long usage. We remained here several days, spending our time visiting the city, and to the theater and the different curiosities that Richmond affords. My father came to see me here but stayed only two days and left at the same time that we got orders to move. In obedience to the order we moved seven miles from Richmond to the neighborhood of Laurel Hill.

Here we pitched our camp in a pleasant old field; this camp was called Camp Mary. We had lain idly in camp for two or three days when we received a most disagreeable order which was to go to work throwing up fortifications, breastworks, &c. Our Brigade was divided into two parts, and we took it day about in the trenches. Now I tell you, this work is anything but fun. One of you home guards look at us poor fellows, sweat rolling down their sun burned cheeks, scorching sun pouring down in full vigor on the partly naked bodies of our brave soldiers. Look at them as with sheer dreariness that are wont to drop down to sleep, and tell me why you would like to fill their places. You would certainly stain your white kid gloves and get some Virginia clay on your snow white pants and your beautiful Saxon complexion would certainly take a deeper and darker color. Oh you young dandified monkeys, Second Chesterfields, this is an age more fitted for the Blount Norman than the prim "François." Enough of this.

We remained here for two weeks, and threw up a line of breast works that will remain for centuries as a memorial of our handiwork. At the end of this time our hardest sufferings began. In accordance with our orders we broke up camp and marched to Richmond. Here I met with a considerable misfortune. My boy, Jesse, took sick and I was compelled to leave him behind a short time. When we reported at Richmond we were ordered to the depot on the Gordonsville road. Here we took the cars and made sail-ho for the valley made memorable by Jackson's exploits. After travelling all day we reached Gordonsville and I may tell you here, this was the last riding we did for a long time. We encamped in a very pleasant grove in Gordonsville that night, hungry and tired, but I managed to get a good supper from one of the surrounding houses by paying an exorbitant price. The next morning rations of the best crackers we had ever had were issued to us and we received orders to march.

We left Gordonsville and marched over what I thought a very hilly country, about seven or eight miles. I was carrying a knapsack full of clothes and I can inform you it made no addition to my speed. We at length arrived at our halting place and some of us had made us tents of poles and bushes, and some of blankets and oil cloths. When we were ordered to move our camp about half a mile westward, behold the inconstancy of a soldier's life, the change and disappointment he undergoes, the privations he endures, all for the sake of his country, the spot we were ordered to move to was entirely free from woods, with the exception of an apple orchard and seemed to resemble a tremendous potato patch, for it was a continued succession of hills, very lofty, and grand and sublime in appearance.

Here was the whole of Longstreet's corps bivouacked on these hills, the azure light of thousands of camp fires sent their ruddy hues toward the skies. The whole landscape, as far as the eye could reach was illuminated by this succession of lights, and by night the scene lent an additional enchantment to the view. This enchanting scene was enlivened by numerous bands of marshal music that sounded forth on the still night breeze, its brazen melodies, and lent an additional luxury to the already enchanting scenery. Look over those hills and you will see the whole of Longstreet's invincible corps sitting, reclining and sleeping on the grassy hillsides. Look at the self-devotion, the patriotism of our noble soldiers as they assemble to vindicate the rights and honor of our oppressed country, and be thankful to an omnipotent God that you live in such a land.

We established ourselves on the summit of one of these hills and lay here a week and I can positively say that I ate more beef and flour that week than I ever did in any two previous to it. Our cooking was truly of an original style. We had no cooking utensils with us, but we invented substitutes by taking flat rocks and heating them to broil our beef upon. You would be surprised at the delicate flavor this type produced, and our plan for cooking flour was still more original. We poured water into the barrel of flour and each one grabbed in and made up his own dough; then some drew it out into a long string and twisted it around sticks to cook before the fire; some made ash cakes, and some more ingenious still, got flat boards and succeeded pretty well in making decent hoecakes. At length however, and to our regret, we received orders to pull up stakes and move.

But by the way, I forgot an expedition, or rather a skirmish we had, at Malvern Hill while at Camp Mary, and I will relate it here before proceeding to our more difficult labors. While in camp at Laurel Hill our pickets below Malvern Hill reported the Yankees advancing, and we were marched out to meet them and oppose their farther progress, but the Yankees, after driving in our pickets, stopped at Malvern Hill and established themselves there, which was about seven miles from our encampment. Gen. Longstreet determined to take the hill and for that purpose we, Evan's Brigade, were sent forward to drive in the enemy's pickets. We left camp in battle trim, with three day's rations, and marched within two miles of Malvern Hill, and we then deployed at two paced apart and advanced on the Yankee pickets. We marched these two miles through the thickest kind of black-jacks and wood, but the Yankee pickets getting wind of us fled, leaving guns, ammunition, knapsacks, and everything to us, but we could not remove any of them as we were still advancing on the enemy.

After getting through the woods we came upon an open old field with woods of Malvern Hill on the other side. Just as we got on the edge of the wood, it being then about dusk, our guide a Cavalryman, and by the by, a brave man, spied a Yankee come galloping through the field. He deliberately got off his horse, took aim through the crack of the fence, and fired, but his gun misfired and the Yankee wheeled and rode away, but the fellow belonging to the picket, and not knowing that they had been driven in, thought his own men had fired at him through mistake, and he rode back up the road to us. Our guide rode out in the road to meet him, and when he came up familiarly addressed him and after holding some conversation with him, he asked the Yankee if he ever saw a Rebel. The Yankee answered no, and our guide then bursting out into a horse-laugh, and clapping the fellow on the shoulder, said, "Well, old buck, you see one now. You belong to me. Come along with me or I'll spile your bacon." It is needless to say, the Yankee was completely astounded.

After this little incident, we marched out into the middle of the old field and laid down the grass and lay here for an hour or so. Our Colonel sent one Company, Capt. Culps, forward to the woods on the side of the road. They had hardly reached there when a company of Yankee Cavalry came riding along. At first they mistook us for friends, but, on approaching nearer, and perceiving their mistake, they fired and wheeled, but we fired into them, and found four

Yankees dead on the road, besides several wounded. As the Yankees ran back the whole of Gadberry's Eighteenth Regiment fired at them and dropped some more. The Yankee Forces at Malvern Hill, on hearing of our advance, evacuated the hills and we took possession. The same night we marched two miles back and bivouacked for the night, but we were kept at this bivouac for two days before we returned to Camp Mary, so ended this expedition.

To return. Now commenced a series of the hardest marches on record. We took up line of march from Gordonsville and marched in the direction of Orange C. H. We travelled the entire day until night, usurped the rule of the day, the men groaning under their knapsacks, and toiling along with feeble steps. At night we were sleep as soon as we touched the ground. I, fortunately left my knapsack behind with Jesse, and had only my blanket to carry. This I twisted and strung over my shoulders like a Scottish Plaid, being the easiest way of carrying it. We lived along our marches on a small ration of bacon and hard crackers, so hard it took rocks to break them, and occasionally we got some roasting ears and green apples, but such things were scarce. We marched on an average of twenty miles a day, but often we had to go very thirsty. I found myself as able, altho young, to stand the march as well as anyone in the company.

That night we sometimes halted, and again sometime marched on 'till near morning, when halted we tumbled down on the spot we were halted at, and, after building a little fire, and eating a scanty supper, roll up in our blankets, and sleep as soundly as if all was peace. Rain may come and drench you, yet, sleep still holds her own. This then was our daily routine. As soon as day dawns again we are on the march. Some point must be gained at every hazard, and every nerve is strained to do so. Pope and his retreating Army retreat steadily before us, occasionally he gives our advance guard a skirmish. At length we crossed the Rapidan River, the enemy still retreating before us. On crossing the Rapidan we were formed in line of battle and advanced through several old fields in battle line, but no enemy appearing in view we again took to the file.

Now, the Rapidan having been crossed – the race was for the Rappahannock, we kept steadily on day after day, past the well fought and victorious battlefields of Cedar Run, until we arrived in the neighborhood of the Rappahannock, and here the enemy seemed determined to make a stand and dispute the passage of the river. We had now been about twenty days on the march continually. The enemy now drew up his artillery on this side of the river, and threw his pontoon bridges across to facilitate his retreat, the next morning after we arrived in the neighborhood of the Rappahannock River, by day dawn, Gen. Evans formed his Brigade in battle order and advanced on the enemy's batteries. We marched over several wheat fields, and being supported by a Detachment of the celebrated Washington Artillery from New Orleans, we pressed forward into range of the enemy's cannon.

The Washington Artillery got up to the top of the hill and opened the ball, then commenced one of the fiercest artillery duels ever fought. We were about 100 yards behind the Washington Artillery and in full range of the enemy's guns. The shells fell around us as thick as hail; the air above our heads was fairly rent with the shrieks of the cannon balls and shells bursting, ricocheting, and whizzing amongst us. The roar of seventy-five pieces at once was truly dreadful, strange to say, we had lost few men so far, but we were lying exposed to every shot, and Gen. Evans, seeing this rode up to us and swore he would take the Yankee battery. He ordered the Halcomb Legion to charge it, and we to follow next. We had an open field to cross, and the enemy seeing this, directed their fire at us and hurled rains of grape, canister, shrapnel and shells at us. Men were falling thick but we charged up the hill, shouting like demons but lo ! the enemy had fled, crossed river, taken up his bridges, and established his battery on a hill on the other side of the river, and now, being out of our reach, poured their fire into us.

We were ordered to lie down on the side of the hill, and there we lay for eight hours beneath a scorching sun, partially shielded by the hill from the enemy's fire, which flew over us like rain, about three feet above our heads, and occasionally dropped among us.

The enemy last found our whereabouts and moving their batteries raked the side of the hill we were lying on, killing and wounding several at the first discharge. We shifted around to the other side of the hill and laid there awhile, when Gen. Evans came up and ordered us to retreat to a piece of woods a short distance back. We were again compelled to cross this old field, and in view of the full fire of the Yankees, but we reached the woods with slight loss. Here we remained until night, and the enemy ceased firing and resumed their retreat. We advanced to the hill we had driven the Yankee battery from and found several dead Yankees and a quantity of commissary. After this severe shelling, and, having buried our dead, and cared for our wounded, resumed the pursuit of the Yankees.

Our Regiment was particularly fortunate in this instance, while the Halcomb lost about sixty in killed and wounded, we had only about six. We marched the next day after the shelling higher up the Rappahannock to the bridge over it, but found this bridge defended by the enemy. We stopped here one day while our pickets kept up a continual scattering fire with the Yankees across the river. The Yankees burned the bridge and seemed determined to prevent our crossing, but here Gen. Stonewall Jackson performed one of those quick evolutions for which he was so famous. About dark one night, leaving the artillery on our side to keep up a fire on the enemy at the bridge, we drew off and marching behind the hills and woods, eluded the sight of the Yankees and making a forced march to a ford about twelve miles down the river, we crossed over, the enemy still thinking we confronted them at the bridge.

The next morning our artillery withdrew and the enemy discovered the ruse played upon them and again commenced a retreat. Our pursuit was hotter than ever. Often we came across a dead Yankee laying in the road, and broken guns, knapsacks and overcoats became more numerous than ever. It was evident that Pope could not go much further without turning to give us battle, and it proved to be a battle worthy of our expectations, and as severe as contending mortals can make it."

"SECOND BATTLE OF MANASSAS..."

> Filled with expectations now, and with memories of death among his troops, but more death among the Federal troops, Samuel felt more emboldened. He had survived enemy fire over his head at a level of only three feet, for eight hours. He and his men had defeated Yankees, chased them after the battle and captured one in a folly of wartime confusion. He had met his first protracted battle and had prevailed, much as he had thought it might be in the quiet nights of the marshes of Kiawah. Along the Carolina coastal islands, he had practiced for this time of glory.
>
> Mickey Beckham

"On Wednesday evening, August 27th, we arrived in the neighborhood of Manassas. On arriving at the little station of Gainesville we were drawn into line of battle after double quick, but crossing only a short distance farther before we bivouacked for the night. On Thursday, the day following, we lay still listening to our picket's stray shots and to the occasional booming of big guns. On Friday we arose considerably refreshed and marched up in reach of the enemy shells that now commenced falling thick and fast. We lay in the woods a short distance from the enemy's line, watching the flying shells as they passed over us, seething, whistling, literally plowing the air, the loud shriek of the flying shells, the dull whiz of the great cannon, with the disappearing cry of wounded mortals, fairly rent the air. Our pickets in front were continually popping away at those of the enemy, while every now and then we would hear the loud shout of Regiments as they would charge upon the enemy, firing like a cane brake on fire, and shouting like demons. All day we lay and listened to these discordant sounds, knowing that our time would soon come to mix in with the general medley. As evening approached the firing became still hotter. Brigade after Brigade hurried to engage in the general revelry.

A short while before dusk Gen. Evans rode up to our Brigade and ordered us to advance. We formed a line and the General ordered us to double quick, and thus we went through bushes, over hills, &c., for half a mile, when we came upon a farm house all around which was strewn with dead bodies. A short distance from this house Benbons Regiment, the 23rd S.C. Vol. being on the left of the brigade was charged upon by a regiment of Yankee Cavalry. Our fellows stopped steady, poured a destructive fire into the charging cavalry, emptying nearly every saddle, and throwing them into the utmost confusion. Those that left immediately wheeled and fled, followed by the exultant shouts of our victorious boys.

While advancing, a stray ball struck W. A. Parker of our company inflicting a wound that proved mortal in a short time. We kept steadily on, waded a deep creek, until we came in view of Gen. Law's Brigade of Alabamians where we halted in a corn field and remained there half the night, wringing wet and shivering with cold. About midnight a rumor reached us that the enemy were trying to get into our rear and Gen. Evans ordered us back to the farm house where we spent the remainder of the night. All night long the pickets kept us a constant firing, indicating that the enemy still confronted us. We all knew that the following day would be an eventful one for some of us, aye, a fatal one. The 30th of August dawned and ushered in a glorious day for our young Confederacy, - one that will ever be remembered in the annals of history, and one whose fame shall never pass into oblivion.

As the day dawned, cannon after cannon boomed forth their iron hail, and the increased firing showed plainly the fierceness of the battle. Regiment after Regiment advanced to the contest. We lay for over half the day listening and watching the contest, and still no orders for us to advance. But at length, the order came. Gen. Evans ordered us to advance, and the whole Brigade started forward in as pretty a line as they had ever formed on dress-parade. We advanced first across a little open space, or small strip of old field, and on entering the woods on the other side the shells came flying over us in close proximity. Gen. Evans ordered us to lie down until the shells passed over us. As I lay down a shell came whizzing over me, about a foot over my head and fell right at my heels, but fortunately it did not explode.

We got up then and charged forward in a good line, through the woods, over the dead and wounded men, shouting like demons. After passing through the woods we entered on a thicket of cedars and here the enemy sent their great shots in perfect hurricanes, crushing and maiming man after man.

On entering a little clump of black-jacks, grape, canister, shrapnel, fairly rattled amid the trees. Here we lost very heavily, the man by my side was killed dead on the spot; our gallant Colonel, Ex-Gov. Means, fell pierced with a ball through the breast while gallantly cheering us on. It seemed strange how a man could escape, still we pressed resolutely on, and, on clearing the woods at Mrs. Chinn's house, we came in full sight of the enemy drawn up in good line, and showing their leaden missiles upon us, the red uniforms of Col. Duryea's New York Knaves, shining prominent in the ranks, with a shout that sounded loud above the cannons roar, we charged forward on the run, firing and loading as fast as possible. The Yankees did not await to lock bayonets with us, but turned and fled precipitately, still keeping up a desultory fire.

While giving our whole attention to the fleeing foe, a regiment of Yankees suddenly drew up line, in a few yards from us on our left, and poured in a destructive fire. And now my turn came, for it was here, while busy loading my rifle, that a ball from the enemy came whizzing through my thigh. My first thought was to look at it, but there was so much blood on my leg that I could not distinguish the wound. The balls continued to fly around me, knocking up the dirt all around me, and I was in imminent danger of getting another one.

I got up and found I could walk a little, and hobbled about five steps back and lay down (Hors de Combat).

The battle continued with unabated fury, grape shells, shot, and Minnie Balls were plowing the air around me, and at that time I was suffering acute pain from my leg. My leg seemed to be numbed all over. Still, with a dull kind of pain thrilling through it. Several other wounded were lying near me. It was while lying here that someone came and lay down beside me saying, "We are friends now if we have been enemies." I did not understand him, in fact, I did not take any notice of him, but I saw he had on a Yankee uniform, which a great many of our men wore, and I supposed him one of our men. I lay still sometime without speaking to him, examining my leg, but having finished I asked him to what regiment he belonged. He replied, "I belong to the 24th Ohio." You are a Yankee then, says I. "Yes," he replied, "but I am tired of this d_____d War, and won't fight any more." I told him I would not trust a Yankee no further than I could see, and demanded his gun, which he complacently delivered, remarking, "It is loaded." I turned him over to our soldiers on their return.

I lay here where I was wounded until the battle ended, which was about half hour after I got wounded. The Yankees were thoroughly whipped. It seemed that the field of Manassas was peculiarly unfortunate for them. As the retreating foe disappeared in the distance I got up on my legs again and commenced to hobble along. I found myself very weak and stiff, just able to limp along, but I assure you it afforded me infinite satisfaction as I knew when I could walk that my leg was not broken.

I hobbled up to Mrs. Chinn's house about one hundred yards from where I was wounded and there I fortunately met one from our company, William Clark, who kindly assisted me, bound up my leg and gave his blanket and oil cloth to me. I will never forget this kindness. He evinced a warm heart and showed a brotherly feeling as soldiers should, for his comrade-in-arms. Poor fellow. He afterwards received his death wound on the field of Sharpsburg. I went into the cellar of the house and lay down for the night, perfectly easy and contented. I felt really happy on my own account, but exceedingly anxious on theirs. I got a soldier to fill my canteen with water and I used that simple, but most healing restorative, on my wound, just pouring it on the spot to keep the fever out of it. I finally got a young Virginia Doctor to bind up my leg and I felt very comfortable the rest of the night.

Capt. Avery, my uncle, who was looking on the battle field for me, found me about twelve o'clock that night in good spirits, and left me, promising to have me carried off in the morning, which he did. I considered myself truly fortunate in getting into the cellar, for it not only rained, but a night amid the dead and dying is not very pleasant. I was partially shielded from the discordant sounds of the wounded and dying, but I heard sufficient to appall the ear of the most hard-hearted stoic.

Discordant sounds rent the air, yells, shrieks, piteous groans and cries of suffering reached the ear on every side. It is truly horrible to witness the mangled bodies of the unfortunate combatants, limbs off, bodies half shot away, features awfully disfigured, &c., all wrapped up in the robe of death. The features were variously marked, some wore the stern aspect of battle, even in death, some presented pictures of despair, some of reckless determination, some of fright, and still some of calmness and self satisfaction truly sublime. Some were smiling in death, seeming to realize that old and patriotic, but romantic maxim, "'Tis sweet to die for one's Country." Peace be to their ashes, a soldier's fate. How wonderfully sudden, how apparently awful.

I spent the night very comfortably, in fact, I slept tho you may think it strange but I did. Morn at last appeared, damp, hazy, chilly, the smoke of battle yet hovered in Manassas, on the battle field, and the bodies of ten thousand dead be spotted the face of nature. The Sun of Austerity never shown on a more desolate scene. About 11 o'clock my uncle came after me and I was carried out on a litter, placed in a wagon with three others of my Regiment, and we were hauled off the battle field to the camp hospital. I would not go in the hospital, but with Lieuts. Logan and Moore, and my cousin W. Dunovant, all wounded, we put up a shanty and stayed in the woods. We had a couple of servants, Noah for one, and did very well.

We lay here 3 or 4 days, when we were carried to Warrenton, and here we hired a little private house and put up for good. I cannot pay too great a tribute to the ladies of Warrenton, Virginia. We were treated with every kindness by these noble hearted women. We were supplied with everything which comfort could demand, and our comforts extended even to luxuries, and their continued solicitude and watchful presence threw a hale of joy over our suffering. The aged, but kind hearted old ladies, as well as the beautiful and accomplished, young damsels, united in their mutual efforts for our comfort. God bless and forever protect them. Let no man ever speak disparagingly of the ladies of Warrenton, for they are models as Patriots and as Ladies. I will ever uphold them.

We remained in Warrenton about ten days when we hired a man for 40 dollars to take us to Rapidan station in an old rough wagon without springs. This was our only plan to get home. We were two days in getting to Rapidan station, but finally reached the desired spot. Here we mounted in an old horse cart and went to Gordonsville, Virginia. Here, to my inexpressible joy, I met my father on his way after me. I found but little difficulty in getting passports for home, and in a week from that day I was safely lodged at home, and in six or eight weeks recovered from my wound entirely. The next year I got a discharge and went to the State Military Institution at Columbia but I am now on the (—illegible—) again, having left school."

SAMUEL'S DISMISSAL FROM THE ARSENAL

The young man, a teenager in years but a man made much older in such a short time, is wounded at Manassas. He sees death now in large numbers and writes about it beautifully, if indeed death on a battlefield can be "beautiful." Samuel looks into the face of friend and foe alike and gives poetry to their masks. He is about to be discharged from the field, but he measures ways to get back into the military and the war, incurring discipline and dismissal from his authorities in Columbia, SC.

Mickey Beckham

"Events occurring in the interval when Samuel Catawba Lowry returned home after being wounded at the Second Battle of Manassas, to the time of his reenlistment in the Confederate Army.

Samuel C. Lowry, after recovering from his wound, was discharged from the army on account of being under age. He was then sent to the Arsenal, a military school in Columbia, S. C., which building is now used as the present Governor's Mansion. After being there about three months, his youthful ardor and patriotism prompted him to attempt to organize a company of volunteers among the cadets. The Commandant, hearing an intimation of this, had the cadet corps drawn up in line on the campus and asked that all who were implicated in this movement make it known. Samuel C. Lowry stepped forward and declared himself the leader, asking his followers to step out from the ranks. Twenty-six responded. All were dismissed from the school. Sam then went to Ebenezer, near Yorkville,

S. C. and stayed at the home of his maternal grandfather, Edward Avery. With his followers he attempted to organize a cavalry company, but failing to secure the requisite number, abandoned the idea, and he and three of his companions joined Company F, 17th S.C. Regiment, commanded by Colonel F. W. McMaster. Of the four who cast their lot in with this company, only one ever returned." (Mrs. Sumter L.) Willie M. Lowry/s/

BOYS THAT LEFT THE ARSENAL IN SEPTEMBER 1863:

1. S. Catawba Lowry — Yorkville, SC
2. G.F.L.A. Massey — Ebenezerville
3. J. Young Goodlett — Greenville
4. R. Lide Burns — Greenville
5. Waddy Thompson — Greenville
6. Thomas S. Hughes — Greenville
7. G. W. Smith — Greenwood, Abbeville District
8. L. F. Connor — Cokesbury
9. J. W. Mays — Cokesbury
10. A. McQueen Salley — Orangeburg
11. Jacob S. Felder — Willow Swamp Orangeburg District
12. C. W. McMorries — Newberry, CH
13. Julius A. Carlisle — Santuck PS-Union District
14. Lewis C. Thompson — Liberty Hill, Kershaw
15. Willedge Galphin — Augusta, Ga.
16. John D. Harrison — Ridgeway, Fairfield
17. Lawrence W. O. Hear — Charleston, SC
18. Robert W. Vaux — Charleston, SC
19. John Ball — Charleston, SC
20. P. G. Stoney — Charleston, SC
21. J. E. Edwards — Columbia, SC

Subsequent to this left:
A. E. Browning   Charleston, SC
Joseph Huger   Charleston, SC
Grange Coffin   Charleston, SC
William Lucas   Charleston, SC

DIARY BY S. C. LOWRY OF COMPANY F. 17TH REGIMENT S.C.V. - COMMENCED ON SULLIVAN'S ISLAND, THIS 22ND DAY OF JANUARY, 1864

"GLADLY WELCOMED BY OLD COMRADES IN ARMS..."

> *Samuel left the warmth of York District and went again to another haven of beauty in his state, Charleston. By this time, he was uncomfortably aware that the northern troops were more into the deep south than he had seen. The Union forces were pounding Fort Moultrie, Fort Sumter and Charleston from the sea with Samuel and his company receiving the damage to the point of ignoring the whistling bombs on many days. They were becoming used to a siege, breaking out often to chase Yankee forces around the city. They reveled when one of their own ships, a blockade runner, foundered and lost its cargo in the surf; they "rescued", pickles, shoes, blankets, oranges and whiskey. The soldier men were being boys again, stealing, trading, buying, bartering, laughing; it would only be a respite.*
>
> *Mickey Beckham*

"Jan. 22nd. This is my first day in camp since the second battle of Manassas. Am gladly welcomed by my old comrades in arms. A warm and pleasant day. Spend my time reviewing the Island and our fortifications, with an occasional stroll along the seaside for shells.

Jan. 23rd. Another pleasant day. Nothing of interest occurred.

Jan. 24th. Sunday. We walked down the Island and got within Ft. Moultrie to review her defenses. Find them remarkably strong, 15 inch guns pointing from every embrasure, ready to belch forth destruction to the heralding foe. Got a splendid view of Ft. Sumpter and the Yankee works on Morris Island. Sumpter is awfully battered.

One side is a pile of ruins, yet her glorious flag floats in haughty defiance over her now hallowed ground. May she ever be as she is now - triumphant. The Yankees throw an occasional shell over to our Island but generally keep up a continual bombardment of Charleston. Return along the beach to camp.

Jan. 25th. A lively and rather cruel sea breeze has sprung up. Drilled twice today.

Jan. 26th. Similar to yesterday. Had several nice games of ball &c.

Jan. 27th. On guard today. Posted at the camp. A very pleasant day and my guard duty was comparatively light. A stray bomb goes whizzing into the city every now and then.

Jan. 28th. Sleep and rest today from my guard duty of yesterday. Get some fresh beef for dinner, the first meat we have received since our arrival, issuing nothing but meat to the soldiers. Light fare. This evening the enemy have commenced an unusually severe shelling of the city and occasionally drop a shell at Moultrie or Sumpter. There goes a bomb plowing the air and shrieking like fury, now, to the city. We have gotten used to them now and they do not even draw a casual remark from the men. Leon Massey and Hughes on guard today. Their first time.

Jan. 29th. All night long the roar of Yankee cannon is heard and is still going on today. Old Sumpter is the subject of their wrath. We can see every shot as it strikes on her walls. The dust flying in columns from their stroke. The enemy occasionally threw a shell into the city and one or two into Moultrie. All quiet in camp.

Jan 30th. The bombardment of Sumpter continues. Somewhat severer than yesterday.

Jan. 31st. Sunday again. Have Regimental inspection today. The bombardment still goes on but not so severely. All quiet in camp. Spend our time today reading and writing.

Feb. 1st. A general inspection and review of the regiment is made this morning by Gen. Beauregard's Aide. We number about 500 men all told. The enemy keep up a lively shelling of Sumpter. All quiet in Camp.

Feb. 2nd. Last night a steamer attempted to run the blockade and, in fact, succeeded, but unfortunately ran aground abreast Ft. Moultrie on the beach. All was now hurry and confusion on board the boat for they knew that as soon as the Yankees could see her they would knock her to pieces. Consequently, all hands commenced unloading, pulling boats pitching overboard barrels, boxes, &c. to wash ashore. Our picket guard on the beach pitched in promiscuously, grabbing for themselves shoes, blankets, oranges, pickles, whiskey, &c.

At daylight the rumor reached camp and crowds of men rushed to the beach eager to get a share of the spoils. Some succeeded in getting something, but soon a guard was posted and the things claimed by the owners, but a great many had been beforehand and skedaddled with their spoils, and, as you would know, such things that were eatable were immediately consumed, but alas for the poor steamer, as soon as the hovering mists began to recede before the coming light of day the Yankees spied her and commenced firing. At first wide, but gradually improving until she was fairly riddled and knocked to pieces.

All day the whiz and shriek of shells are heard and in dangerous proximity to us. It was truly a grand sight to stand off and look at the effect of each shot, first the enemy's batteries on Morris Island fired, and then the three iron-clad, turreted Monitors would steam up and pour forth a stream of lead on the devoted steamer. They wounded and probably killed several of our men who ventured too close. They are firing now at this moment with redoubled severity. I bought two pair of shoes today that had been taken from the steamer, one pair for twenty dollars, the other for fifteen.

Feb. 3rd. The roar of cannon is the first thing heard this morning. They fired all night long at the steamer. Today is my turn for guard again and it happened that I was detailed for guard at Moultrie in the very course of shot and shell from the Yankees. We left camp and started for our post, and as soon as we got in range of shell we crept along by the breast-works as fast as possible until we reached the bombproof.

All day long here the shot and shell whizzed directly over our heads, but we were shielded by the bomb proof and laughed at the danger. A great many struck our bomb proof but did no great harm, but safe as we were, we found the place very uncomfortable, on account of the sand continually falling in our eyes, and a part of us resolved to risk a little for the sake of comfort, consequently we came out of the bomb proof and took our seats behind the breast works.

We sat here a long time, gazing at the shells whistling by, and at last decided we were perfectly safe here, but we were too quick in our decision, for scarcely had we done so when a sixty pound shell fell with amazing force in three feet of us, but fortunately did not burst. If it had done so but few would have escaped.

Night at last came and ushered in a painful scene. A poor woman, a soldier's wife who had come from home to see him, was brought in the bomb proof with one arm shot off and a dreadful wound in the leg. Her arm was immediately amputated and her other wound being dressed, she was sent off to the hospital. The same shell that wounded her killed a man. Another man was also brought in with his arm shot all to pieces. It was also amputated. All night long the Yanks shelled, but their fire was somewhat slackened near day and only an occasional shot was heard in the morning.

Feb. 4th. This morning I was awfully scared by a shell. The firing had ceased for a long time and Sergeant Ruce Workman and myself had gone out to see the Regulars mount guard when Lo! a monitor steamed up, and let loose her bull dogs before we could reach any cover. The ball ripped its way on the water making a noise like a dozen cannon. I squatted behind a little brick wall, or cistern for water, no protection at all from above, but dodging was natural. Ruce fell flat and crawled under the house. On came the shell, and at last with a tremendous fuss exploded within a few yards of us, shattering the pieces of bricks down on us, and giving us an awful jar. Ruce and I immediately left the spot and made clean tracks for the bomb-proofs. As I turned, I saw my boy Henry who had brought me my breakfast, leaving the spot where he had come, also with lightning speed. Shortly after we were relieved and returned to camp, and slept the rest of the day. I bought three pair of shoes today again for $10 a pair.

Feb. 5th. This morning we find that some of our boys had been on the steamer in the night and brought us some pickles, pork and a box of champagne. We purchased several bottles and drank them very speedily as you might suppose. Today everybody is planning to get on the steamer. At night crowds were seen making toward the steamer, which seemed as if the whole Brigade had turned out, but sentinels had been posted and they were all stopped and informed they could not pass. For awhile the boys were raging and swore they would pass anyhow, and some did. The crowd was very large and much excited. At length, Col. Keith was brought out and he addressed the crowd, and appeased them by promising to divide cargo of the ship equally, and they were all satisfied and disbursed.

Feb. 6th. All quiet today. I went down to the steamer this morning but could not get on board. She is torn almost to pieces, one end under water.

Feb. 7th. Go thru the usual camp routine.

Feb. 8th. All still. Spend the day reading and writing.

Feb. 9th. On guard today at camp in place of Sergeant Happerfield, sick.

Feb. 10th. Today I received a letter from home bearing me the grateful news of the birth of another little brother on the 2nd of February.

I am all anxiety to see him, but know that it will probably be a long time before I do see him. Late this evening orders came to prepare three days rations for a march and have full supplies of ammunition. We had no idea as to our destination then, but found out afterwards that a demonstration had been made on John's Island by the Yankees who were reported to be still advancing, and we were ordered to be in readiness to repel the advance, but the Yanks finally concluded that discretion was the better part of valor, and went back to their boats.

Feb. 11th. All quiet today. Nothing to arouse us from the lethargy of camp routine.

Feb. 12th. Very windy today. Waves running high. Some of our boys went to the wreck of the Presto last night after powder but got none.

Feb. 13th. Lay quietly in camp until at dress parade we were surprised by orders received by the Colonel to take up the march and leave our camp for the boat at Mt. Pleasant to proceed to James Island in light marching order. The enemy had made quite a formidable demonstration on John's Island, and we were ordered to Fort Pemberton on James Island to be in readiness to proceed forthwith to John's. We marched to Mt. Pleasant for, and took the steamer there for Dill's Bluff. We were about four hours crossing, caused by the steamer running aground, but at last arrived, landed and bivouacked for the night.

Feb. 14th. Slept very soundly last night, and feeling good spirits. We lie at our bivouac all day, get very tired lying about, but the boys are very merry. Tonight we go back to camp on Sullivan's Island, the enemy having retreated on John's Island.

Feb. 15th. This evening, again orders come to box up and travel this time for some distance and I suppose a permanent move as we take all of our luggage with us. We marched to Mt. Pleasant after dark, took the boat for the Savannah Railroad wharf, run aground once, but got over safely, but bivouacked for the night at our old camp of two years ago (Camp Lee).

Feb. 16th. This morning we take the train and are rapidly borne on the iron track towards Green Pond where we arrived at about three o'clock, and marching about one mile from the railroad, took up quarters for the present and here I am now.

Feb. 17th. Remained in our bivouac here all day, nothing of importance occurring.

Feb. 18th. This morning we left our bivouac for the camp of a cavalry regiment just vacated by them about two miles from our bivouac. Here we found most excellent quarters, nice little cabins ready built for us. They are decidedly the best quarters that we have had since the War began. We spend the day fixing up.

Feb. 19th. Today I took a stroll after wild ducks. Thousands of them are to be found in the neighborhood. We had only our Austrian rifles, and, altho we saw four or five thousand of them, killed none and returned to camp weary and mortified.

Feb. 20th. Took another stroll after ducks today, but they were not to be found today and we vented our rage out on killing blackbirds and one chicken that we bought. Nothing new in camp. We received a large box of meat from the ladies of Yorkville, S. C. and duly appreciated the generous gift.

Feb. 21st. Sunday again. Preaching today by our Chaplain, Mr. Morse. Cousin Willie returned today from home. My boy Henry is very sick today, so much so as to alarm me.

Feb. 22nd. Henry no better this morning, and I resolved to send him home by Capt. Avery who goes home on furlough this morning, having lost his dwelling house by fire a few days previous. The boys put up a gymnasium pole today and it is a source of great amusement to us all. Have general inspection today.

Feb. 23rd. Nothing of importance occurred today.

Feb. 24th. All quiet in camp except the regular drills, and camp routine.

Feb. 25th. Tonight we received marching orders to cook one day's rations and start by sunup in the morning for Stock's Causeway, ten miles distance.

Feb. 26th. We left camp this morning in light marching trim and soon marched over the ten miles of sandy road, without any occurrence of interest, and found on our arrival at our destination (the plantation of Dr. Jerido) that we were brought here to work.

Feb. 27th: Leave our bivouac this morning and marched boldly into the native swamps, through which we were ordered to cut a road for transportation. We went to work cutting down trees, carrying poles to build causeways across marshy places, shoveling dirt, &c. We worked only four hours in the day and have the rest of the day to ourselves.

Feb. 28th. Work again today. Went out this morning to a turkey blind to try and kill a turkey but failed. Nothing new. The boys catch two or three coons.

Feb. 29th. One of company killed a large wild turkey this morning. Work as usual. Not hard.

March 1st. Still at work on the road, nothing new. I bought me a little double barrel shot gun today for thirty five dollars. Coons, Possums, and squirrels are caught in abundance.

March 2nd. Still at work. Today I got permission to come to camp. R. I. Withers arrived to our mess today.

March 3rd. Returned to the company. Find alright and still at work.

March 4th. Today our working detachment was relieved by another portion of the regiment as we returned to camp after a dusty march of ten miles.

March 5th. Nothing new. Spent the day cleaning up.

March 6th. Sunday. Preaching by our Chaplain, Mr. Morse, today. Visit the railroad station and meet two old acquaintances and former school mates on the train. I, Earl and LePrince.

March 23rd. Having failed to keep up my diary on account of the regiment being sent out on detached duty, and not returning to camp, I will begin anew after detailing as briefly as possible our employment during this interval. We were again ordered to Stock's Causeway to work on the breast works, and we have been employed every day since putting up a Fort at Burnett Farm. Work four hours each day with spades, wheel-barrow, &c. and the rest of the day is at our own disposal, which we spent in various ways. Some hunting, fishing, and loafing at camp. We caught a plenty of excellent cat fish and eels, on which we fared sumptuously, and occasionally killed a duck. We are still at work here and will probably be kept here until the Fort is finished. It is reported, and truly I believe, that Gen. Evans has been restored to his command, and Col. McMaster has gone to Richmond to get out of his command, being deadly foes. I will continue my diary from this date."

DIARY BY S. C. LOWRY, CO. "F" 17TH S. C. V. COMMENCED THIS 20TH DAY OF APRIL, 1864

"WE HAVE JUST RECEIVED ORDERS TO PREPARE FIVE DAYS RATIONS..."

In April of 1864 the war takes the turn that Samuel writes about from a front row view. Northern troops under Grant, moving toward Richmond number 120,000. They are promising to end the war against Lee who stands in their way with 64,000 men and more coming.

Samuel is among the "more coming."

Mickey Beckham

"I have just returned from home on furlough of twenty days. Had a very pleasant time. On my way back to my regiment, which I had left in camp at Green Pond, S. C. I learned that they were under way for Wilmington, N. C. and probably thence to Virginia. I immediately then gave chase arriving at Charleston. I spent the night there and took the cars next day for Wilmington. I learned on arriving at this place that I had already outstripped my command and had passed the regiment on the road in the night. A very wet day, raining continually. I halted here to await my regiment which came up in the evening, drenched with rain. Attend the theater this night. Very much pleased with the performance; "Camille", exciting French Tragedy, being the principal act, and a most beautiful dance, (Grand Pas de Due) by two lovely young actresses. An occasional attendance, which by our numerous circumlocution we sometimes manage to enjoy, affords a pleasant recreation to our monotonous entertainment.

April 20th. We are in camp two miles from Wilmington. Will leave in a day or two for Weldon between which place and Tarboro it is reported we are destined for the present to confront Gen. Burnside's demonstration on the Peninsular in anticipation of an attack on Richmond from that direction. We marched to Wilmington to take the cars for Weldon, but the order was countermanded and we returned.

April 21st. We are now located in splendid quarters, just evacuated by Martin's N. C. Brigade, but we expect to leave them soon. This evening orders arrived to leave for Weldon again, and we again marched to Wilmington, and again as before the order was countermanded, and we returned cursing the inconstancy of a soldier's life. It is now thought we will be kept here sometime. The rest of the Brigade has gone on to Weldon. Gen. W. S. Walker is now in command of it. Vice Gen. Evans, lately injured by a fall from a buggy. Our present camp is one of the most pleasant that we ever occupied.

A short distance from us is one of the most beautiful little rivers that I ever beheld. Tonight our mess went down to have a sail in the canoe. The night shone resplendent by the ruddy beams of the moon, and was one of the most lovely that I ever beheld. The dark blue canopy above, studded with stars, unutterably bright, illuminated by a fair lunas beams, was one that would compare with the brightest skies that ever blessed a tropical June. California celebrated for it's illumined skies, Cuba blessed with the rays of a tropical clime, could not surpass it. Enough.

The river, Ah O'Helicon, am I a paltry subaltern in the art "de" descriptions can I do justice, aye, even described so exalted a subject, I fear not. It would take something more than a man of letters, aye, even a poet. This lovely stream, pearls along its transparent waters amid the towering forest like a silvery beam athwart the darken clouds, bounded by the most luxuriant of lowland vegetation on its banks; crystal waves of most astounding transparency, all combined to render it one of nature's brightest gems. No one with a love for the works of nature could have failed to admire it. How could he pass it unobserved. Sailing over its still waters by moonlight, inhaling the delicious fragrance of its flower covered banks, listening to the gentle murmurs of the waves, the musical whistle of the still night breeze, varied by the hoarse growl of the native crocodile, and the answering call of the shrill throated whippoorwill, all point out the favoring hand of nature.

We sailed up this river enjoying ourselves by playing tricks on one another's boats. Enough. This is East River two miles from Wilmington, N. C. or at least this is the name we hear it called.

April 22nd. Last night we were aroused about twelve o'clock by the long roll (of drums), and we rolled out of bed much to our dissatisfaction, pulled on our clothes in a hurry, ran out and fell in ranks with guns and accoutrements, but it proved to be a false alarm, so far as we were concerned, since we did not leave camp. But the Yankees landed about eight miles below us and burned the N. C. salt works, retiring as soon as they had burned the works.

Nothing new today. We catch some fish out of my beautiful river. Co. A. is sent to Charleston to guard some prisoners, captured by Gen. Hoke at Plymouth. We have just received orders to prepare five days rations and proceed to Tarboro to conduct the aforesaid prisoners, 2,500 in number, to Charleston, S. C. on their way to prison in Georgia. All getting ready, leave in half hour to take the cars at Wilmington for Goldsboro.

April 23 to May 1st. We are again at camp, having been for the last eight days on the road with prisoners. We left Wilmington about dusk on the 23rd and travelled all night, reaching Goldsboro next morning about eight o'clock. Stayed here only a few moments when we ran through on the same train for Tarboro, reaching there late in the evening. I found Tarboro to be one of the prettiest places that I ever saw, and, from appearances, seemed to be a place of wealth. Beautiful residences, surrounded by shady yards, bounded the principal street.

The town is situated on the Tarr River, a beautiful stream, and on the whole the place presents a very favorable view to a stranger's eye. Late, about dark, we marched thru town across the river and took up our bivouac on the opposite bank about one mile from town. Here we lay for two days, waiting for the Yankees to be brought up from Plymouth. At last they came in sight marching along, guarded by the Halcomb Legion. They were well uniformed and a stout body of men, but tired and awful hungry. They offered gold rings, five dollar pieces, &c. for a little piece of bread. Our fellows did not hesitate to trade with them, but got knives, pipes, rings &c for bread. The Yankees were marched into a bull pen, formed by our guard, and rations given out to them. A strong guard was mounted and kept on all night.

The next day Company A and Company F were sent off to take charge of a detachment of prisoners. We had 680 in numbers and marched thru town and took the cars from Tarboro. Forty prisoners and five guards being put into a box car. We were very much crowded, and such cursing (for they were without exception the most wicked set I ever had anything to do with) they were a very impudent set, New York and Pennsylvania troops. Real black Republican Abolitionists, we made them walk straight and soon got them to fear to disobey any orders. They were ultra in their political principals, but actually they did not know what they were fighting for. They regard Grant as Honorable and are confident of his success against Lee this summer. We have little trouble with them beyond tedious guard duty, and in due time arrived at Charleston where we were relieved by some other command and returned to camp glad the trip was over.

May 1st. Today is the Sabbath, sleep all morning to regain my lost sleep. This evening hear an excellent sermon by our Chaplain, Mr. Morse. Find a great relief in getting something better to eat than hard crackers which we had been eating for the last eight days.

May 2nd. Nothing new in camp. Drill today, the first in a long time.

May 3rd. On guard in camp today; orders to conduct some prisoners (deserters) to prison in Wilmington, which I did without trouble.

May 4th. This morning we are, that is, Company H and F ordered to report to Wilmington for Provost Duty. We were quartered in an old brick building, formerly the town poor house. I am detailed with the men for guard. As soon as we reach quarters ordered to go to the guard house for duty. Duty heavy, but a little more life about it than usual. Attend the theater as guard, and patrol the town at night. Nothing occurred worth mentioning.

May 5th. Relieved from guard this morning. Sleep all morning. Go to theater tonight. Nothing new.

May 6th. All quiet. Still on Provost duty in the city. The big fight is begun in Virginia between Lee and Grant. The enemy advancing on Richmond from every direction. Terrific battle going on. Great excitement prevails, except amid the soldiers who look on the thing as a necessary consequence, and thank their stars they are not as yet participant. But we look for orders constantly to leave for the scene of action.

May 7th. The battle still progressing. No orders for us yet, nothing new. Hard up for something to eat. Living on corn meal and spoiled bacon. We have just received the lamentable news of the death of Gen. Micah Jenkins of Yorkville. He was the pride of S. C. One of her noblest sons and should be consecrated by fame as an immortal hero. I was tenderly attached to him, having been his pupil for three years at the military school of York, and he was a particular friend of the family. Just left home a few days ago and now, alas, he is numbered with the dead. A victim to Northern Fanaticism, for he died a glorious death at the head of his brigade on the battle field. He would soon have been Major General and, but for this untoward fate, would in time have reached the very pinnacle of glory. Peace be to his ashes. Calm and quiet may they rest on some vine clad hill of his own beloved Carolina until wafted away by the whispering zephyrs they reach their proper abode in a celestial clime. God grant it so.

May 8th. On guard today, a blockader ran into this port this morning. No news from Virginia. Cornbread and water for my meals today. Two cases of small pox at hospital.

May 9th. Relieved this morning from guard. All quiet today.

May 10th. Col. Miller of 12th Regiment, SCV was killed in the late battle. He was from Yorkville and a brave, courageous officer. So far we are entirely victorious in Virginia. The wires were cut by the Yankee raiders and we will get no more news until they are repaired. No news in camp.

May 11th. On guard again today. Three blockaders ran into this port today and four yesterday. Patrol the town tonight.

May 12th. All anxiety to hear from Virginia. Sleep today to recover that lost last night. All quiet in camp.

May 13th. Nothing new.

May 14th. Received some letters from home, the first in four weeks. Very anxious there on my account. News unimportant from Virginia. Wires are down and we can get nothing reliable.

May 15th Sunday. Go to church this morning at St. John's Episcopal church.

May 16th. Nothing new.

May 17th. On guard today, but we have just received orders to prepare four days rations to leave tonight for more stirring scenes. We will probably go to Petersburg, Virginia.

May 18. We are now at Weldon and leave today for Petersburg. We have just heard of our glorious victories at Petersburg, and in North Virginia. Lee over Grant. Beauregard over Butler.

May 19th. We are now in the vicinity of Petersburg, and have heard ours and the enemy's pickets firing all day. Had a terrific battle here two days ago, a complete victory for us. We expect to go into battle at any moment. I am now in one mile of my Grand Uncle John Avery. Gen. Lee has so far whipped old Grant. We got a thorough wetting today from rain.

In coming here on the train we saw the effect of the Yankee raiders on the P. & W. Railroad. Houses burned, track torn up, dead horses, &c. Gen. Walker is now in command of our Brigade, four Regiments all together. This evening we received orders to move to Battery No, 5, along the line of breastworks, about half mile away. We marched out there and hope to stay here awhile for it is a splendid place to fight.

May 20th. Eventful day. Last night about nine o'clock we were ordered to take up line of march immediately and report to Gen. Beauregard's headquarters, 14 miles away. We started and trudged along, awful tired and sleepy, reaching the neighborhood of headquarters about two o'clock in the morning. Just as we got there ours and the Yankee pickets were actively engaged firing very heavily about quarter of a mile distance. We knew that stirring times were coming. We lay down in the woods and slept 'till day soundly. At day-break we marched out to take our position. We proceeded to a line of breast works, and took our position immediately in rear to support another line."

BATTLE OF HOWLETT'S FARM

"WE ARE NOW IN THE VICINITY OF PETERSBURG...."

Samuel wrote, "We knew that stirring times were coming." He was witnessing the spawning of major battles of the Wilderness, May 5-6, Spotsylvania, May 8-12 and Cold Harbor, June 1-3. On June 3 Grant made a mistake that cost 7,000 Union causalities in 20 minutes. In that battle, a Union soldier also recorded his own thoughts, "June 3 1864, Cold Harbor, Virginia. I was killed."

Samuel and his own began a march that took them to a victory under Beauregard where 10,000 men were engaged and 1,500 causalities would be recorded. It was the beginning of the Petersburg siege, a battle that historians now say gave us the same trench warfare that epitomized World War I.

Mickey Beckham

"About ten o'clock in the morning we were ordered to march. We knew not where, but which soon proved itself to be to battle. We passed thru a little thicket of blackjack scrubs into an old field planted with cane, directly in rear of Mr. Howlett's house. Around the house our skirmishers and the Yankees were hotly engaged and we marched up to support them within forty yards of the house. Directly in front of us was our extreme line of fortifications, and about quarter of a mile distance we saw the Yankee line. These were to be taken by us. The Minnie balls began to fall thick and fast around us, and we drew up to the line of breastworks. It soon became known along the line that we were to charge the Yankees in our front, and many a heart quivered and fluttered with excitement, and an instinctive dread of the coming task.

But the firm resolution to do or die beamed upon every countenance. We were anxious for the word to forward, for we felt that the sooner it was over the better we would feel. At last our gallant Colonel McMaster gave the word, "Steady, Forward, Charge," and over our works we leaped, yelling like demons, charging forward at the double quick. Not a man faltered, tho many fell, and on we rushed until we reached the enemy's works, from which we drove them by main force. They ingloriously fled and we poured a parting load into their flying and scattered ranks. Some of our men leaped the breastworks and followed the retreating foe to some distance, but were ordered back. We now quietly lay down behind the works awaiting the enemy's attempt to regain it. They rallied forward and with a shout rushed on toward us, but, alas, they were met with a rain of Minnies from our fellows and fell back, confused and scattered. Again they tried, and met with a similar reception.

Again, the third, they formed a splendid line and came forward in good order, but the old 17th was awake, and farely poured in their balls on their ranks. They wavered, broke, and fled in dismay. Once more they made a feeble attempt to drive us away, but to no purpose, and they finally concluded that discretion was the better part of valor, and gave up their fruitless attempts, but such a rain of shells and balls as they poured on our fellows we never have seen since the second Battle of Manassas.

We were ordered to go to work with our bayonets and throw up breastworks, which we did, but fortunately we got some spades and shovels left by the Yankees, and for awhile spade and shovel were plied as vigorously as our rifles a few minutes before, and a stout breastworks was soon in front of us. A steady fire was kept up between us until night spread her sable curtain over the field of dead. Our front was thickly being spotted with dead Yankees, but our own loss was comparatively trifling. In our company we lost Private William Martin, killed, Lieut. W. S. Moore, wounded in thigh,

Robert Randall, shoulder, I. W. Y. Dixon, ditto, slight. Our success along the whole line was complete and old Butler was cooped still closer under his gunboats. The Yankees loss was estimated at from three to four thousand. Ours about one thousand. So ended the victory of May 20th.

May 21st. Last night the enemy, under cover of darkness, threw up, or dug, some rifle pits about three hundred yards away, and our boys and them have been picking at each other all day, occasionally killing or wounding one. The sun is awful hot. We have no shade, We get some haversacks, canteens &c. from the battlefield.

May 22nd. All night our fellows keep up a constant fire and don't allow us to sleep a bit. The enemy have been making demonstrations on our right and left all day, but are always driven back after sharp fighting. Awful hungry. Can get nothing today but dry corn bread and some ice that we found in an ice house.

May 23rd. We changed our position last night and moved farther to the left. The Yankees discovered it and opened on us with their batteries, and for half-hour such incessant firing I never heard, all to no purpose, for we sheltered ourselves by our breastworks. No harm done, but a great deal of ammunition wasted. Very hot and no shade.

May 24th. Today we lie quiet, tho our pickets keep up a constant racket. Tonight we go on picket.

May 25th. At dark last night we left the trenches for the rifle pits in front for picket. We passed half the night very quietly, but about one o'clock, the firing commenced and was pretty well kept up until daybreak. We could only fire at the flash of the enemy's guns, but two or three were killed. I did not fire often for I wanted to see more than a flash to fire at. We were relieved at daybreak and slept nearly all day in the trenches. Hear good news from Lee's Army. He has been entirely successful so far, but it is saddened by the loss of many friends killed.

May 26th. Today all is quiet so far. I hear sad news of the death on the battle field of my most intimate friend in Lee's Army, but it is not confirmed. (Allen Jones) God grant it is not so. I am glad to say this is a mistake, he is unhurt. Beauregard's whole command here in good spirits, and confident of success. My boy, Henry, comes in every evening to our breastworks to bring me something to eat. I forgot to state in my account of the battle of Howlett's Farm that our Gen. W. S. Walker was wounded and taken prisoner by the enemy. He accidentally rode into the Yankee lines by mistake while going around inspecting our works, and in attempting to escape was wounded and captured.

May 27th to June 10th. During this time I have not been able to keep my book with me, and consequently I cannot give a detailed account of each day's transactions, but will revive the whole as briefly as possible. We are still in the trenches where we have been ever since the battle of May 21st. We have shifted our position several times, but keep in the trenches. One can easily imagine our condition. Rolling in ditches of red clay, with no protection from rain or sun, and a continued series of working details and pickets. Thus it was that we passed the weary, monotonous hours of the long, long days, nothing to read, nothing to do but work, with spade or shovel, or keep a sleepy watch of picket, until aroused from his lethargy by the loud reports of picket firing, he wakes and realizes his danger. Sleep is our only luxury and refuge from labor, and this is coveted by all. Nearly every night we are aroused by our pickets or the enemy's firing. They are in sixty yards of each other and the least movement to the front on either side is the signal alarm.

One morning our whole picket line advanced and a heavy skirmish was the result. We capturing the enemy's rifle pits by a charge, and about two hundred prisoners with a good many fine patented Spencer's Repeating Carbine, but the enemy advanced in heavy form to retake the pits and our boys were reluctantly compelled to yield them up after a stout resistance. Col. Dantzler of 22nd S.C.V. was killed in this charge. Our Regiment was nearly on the extreme right, and our pickets in advancing on the left met many Yankees. These they came upon cooking, completely surprising them. They killed five or six and took two or three prisoners, but had two men wounded in company K, Black Davidson and Alex Lockart.

The right of the line, where our company was, advanced one mile and a half and found not a Yankee, but an awful rugged country. Since this row we have had some hot shellings, and roar of the big guns around us, and the shrill shriek of the answering shells, formed for the time a grand, sublime bout, terrible panorama. Our fare was very rough. Corn bread and bacon, and that very scanty. But we endure cheerfully, and confidently hope the time is not far off when we can realize the scenes set forth in that enchanting song, "When This Cruel War is Over." We have been in the trenches now twenty days without relief and there is no telling how much longer we will stay.

Lee's success is so far uninterrupted. No news from home. Mail irregular. Great excitement prevailed yesterday in Petersburg, caused by the enemy's advancing on the city. It was a force of Yankee Cavalry raiders, five to six thousand strong. They were resisted by the Petersburg militia who fought them manfully, but were compelled to fall back before superior numbers. The Yankees followed and were almost entering the city when Wilson's Brigade came up and drove them back, completely defeating them and saving the city. We received orders to be ready to move and expecting to have gone, but we have not yet.

June 12. All quiet. Rations scarce. Duty hard.

June 13th. Grant reported to be moving around this way, heavy cannonading heard in the distance this morning.

June 14th. Still all quiet, contrary to our expectations. Rations very scarce. Nothing to eat and the duty very hard. Considerable complaining among the men, and they have good cause for complaint.

July 14th. Today one month ago I left off my diary, and in consequence I will have to give another detail of affairs, promiscuously, without reference to date. We remained a day or two after June 14th at Bermuda Hundreds, when it was found out that Grant had changed his base again and was moving his hoards again to Petersburg. This caused considerable excitement and we immediately got ready to move our quarters.

Soon one morning, before day, we abandoned our works, which, in one hour after we left them, were teeming with Yankees, and we marched for Petersburg, where the enemy were already knocking away our works, and had so far been successfully repulsed. As we arrived on the outskirts of town, we could hear the cannons booming forth from the works on the opposite side of town, together with the sharp crack of our rifles. We were not stopped in town a minute, not even to rest, but marched straight thru until we were in the vicinity of our works, when we were halted in a pine grove and bivouacked for the night. Here we remained the greater part of the following day, and I found out that I was in half mile of my Uncle John Avery's house.

My old Aunt Sallie sent us a nice snack of something to eat. The day after we got to Petersburg we marched to the breastworks and took our position just at Mr. Rives house, which the enemy had burned a day or two before in their raid. Here we were to support a battery.

About dark that evening a terrific battle began on our left, boom after boom went from the big guns, intermingled with the most incessant rattle of musketry that I had ever heard. The Yankees were making desperate attempts to take our works, and we could hear distinctly the Yankees shout as they charged, and our boys' defiant yell in return. It was a grand panorama, and to those not engaged, but who expected to be at any moment, it was peculiarly interesting. To add to the excitement we saw crowds of our boys beginning to fall back in our front, and when they came up found out that it was a battery from Macon, Georgia, which had lost its guns. The enemy had succeeded in penetrating our lines here and captured their guns.

This was bad news, and we confidently expected to move forward to retake the works, but no such order came and we remained stationary. Awhile after dark, the firing ceased and we slept the rest of the night. In the morning we marched out and took position in the front line of works, but the works were badly constructed and enabled the enemy to flank fire the whole line so we were compelled to throw up traverses. Here they shelled us all day and killed our Adjutant, J. V. Connor, and another man of Co. A. At dark it was understood that we were to give up this line of works and fall back a short distance and build a new line, and a more contracted one. We had been started out on picket, but were just posted when we were ordered back and immediately commenced leaving the works silently and secretly.

As we got out into the Jerusalem Plank Road, a sharp fight was going on around Taylor's house on top of the hill. We expected to march up to battle every moment, but we lay in the road until nearly day when we fell back to the top of the hill this side of the branch, marching half way between to Rives house, commenced throwing up breastworks, so here it may be said, commenced our life in the ditches.

We worked with a will, and the dawn of day found us behind good breastworks. Our pickets were still in our front, and we could hear them and the Yankees skirmishing. We continued to improve our works until we had them completed. Nothing of importance took place that day, but the morrow was the eventful day. The enemy's sharpshooters began to bother us considerably and they kept busy putting their guns in position all day when they opened their batteries on us, raining shot and shell and between them and the sharpshooters, we lost several men wounded."

"HIS BLOODY CORPSE WAS BORNE AWAY BY OUR AMBULANCE MEN..."

This was the battle in the war that young men who volunteer never imagine. Samuel, through the death of others, was elected a Lieutenant and would become an acting Captain as men fell. He would lie in trenches for days, exchanging deadly fire, "rolling in the clay of the ditches" becoming "as dirty as hogs" and with lice on his body. It would become a stalemate with Union forces, out of impatience and seeking a breakout strategy, building a tunnel packed with explosives under Confederate lines. That strategy was not even looked upon with much promise by Union generals. All of this brought on when Union forces miss their chance to capture Petersburg and cut Confederate rail lines. This siege is to last nine months with Grant having Lee surrounded.

Union troops succeed in blowing a hole so large it becomes a massive crater. Then owing to the complexities and confusion of war, they see 3789 of their own killed, wounded and missing as they rush into the crater while Confederates pour rifle fire down into them from the rim. Confederates lose half as many, 1491 in all. Samuel survives the enormous detonation but engages in combat, much of it hand to hand, with rifle fire so intense bullets from both sides collide in mid air, fusing or splitting. Samuel lasts almost five hours. He is still a teenager on this day June 30, 1864.

Henry Avery looks for Samuel's body among the carnage. He is looking at men piled on top of each other, some in

> *the throes of dying, groaning and crying, some without a face, others disemboweled or without limbs. The most are Northern, among them black troops as well. The stench is incomprehensible to any civilian who has only heard, never witnessed.*
>
> *The young man from York finds his friend and removes from his body and then from his tent, personal belongings including a precious document, the diary you are reading here. This is a family member he has traveled with, waited on; now he begins the process of bringing him home, 300 miles away, back to Yorkville and his family.*
>
> *Ten months later Lee will surrender to Grant, April 9, 1865.*
>
> Mickey Beckham

"This evening at about five o'clock the enemy commenced massing in our front. At first they threw out a skirmish line, but our line, under Major Betgil of 18th, charged them and ran them back. Then they displayed a line a little to our right and drove in our pickets. Shortly after this they threw a line of battle in the edge of a piece of woods, and making them lie down, massed four lines behind them. They then deployed another skirmish line and advanced it forward. It was at this juncture that we lost our much lamented company commander, Lieut. David I. Logan. He ordered the men to keep down their heads for the enemy were sharpshooting fast, and in his zeal for his men, exposed himself when a stray ball struck him square in the forehead killing him instantly. He never groaned, but was dead in a minute. It threw a gloom over every countenance and cast a damper over the whole company.

His bloody corpse was borne away by our ambulance men, which was the last of our lamented Lieutenant. He was an officer and a gentlemen, a man of brilliant intellect, who by his kind heart and gentle ways, had attached himself to every one of us. I can say no more, but his death was a shock so unexpected as to almost overcome my discretion. He is gone, and I trust is with his God in Heaven. Shortly after he had been borne off the enemy began to make furious demonstrations in our front. In a few moments their front line appeared and came forward at double quick, followed by four other lines, seemingly bent on taking our lines, but they did not count the cost.

"Fire" came the word, and our whole line was a sheet of flame. The Yankees in our line began to dwindle down and before they had got in one hundred yards of our works, we turned their tune, for they broke and fled in utter dismay, followed by the shouts and bullets of our victorious boys. Every now and then after the main body had reached the woods, a solitary Yankee would rise and make for the woods, followed by shouts of laughter from our boys. Again the Yankee officers attempted to renew the charge, acting, I must say, with considerable bravery, but forming a line as they did, still they could not prevail on the Yanks to charge us again, who, after two or three more futile attempts, desisted altogether. We had one man in our company wounded by his own gun, E. W. Bridges, finger and thumb shot off. This was our only casualty, while many a Yankee bit the dust in our front.

I do not know the number of the enemy killed or wounded. Dark closed in silently, but in the night the enemy made another charge on our left, but as usual were repulsed. The following day was passed in rest, except occasional shelling and sharp shooting.

This night we were relieved by Field's Division and went back to the rear to rest and clean up for a few days. During this time I was elected Brevet Second Lieutenant in our company. We lived remarkably well on vegetables that we could procure at reduced prices. We stayed back here five days when we again went into the trenches. But in the mean time, we had been engaged in a flank movement under General Matrone succeeded in capturing about 3000 prisoners, two lines of breast works, eight pieces of artillery, with several stands of colors and small arms. We were ordered to support Gen. Matrone's Division and only a part of our Brigade was actively engaged. We went out in front of our breastworks, and lay in supporting distance of Matrone all night, until about daybreak, when we returned to our works perfectly satisfied.

On the following day we went out there again, but this time to throw up breast works, which we did, and with the usual luck of our brigade, marched away at dark, coming back to our old line. We took position about the center of the line, where we found the Yankee line of works in about 200 yards of ours, and a continual sharpshooting was going on all the time. We were in a stone's throw of one another, and thus we have been now for 21 days. We lie here day after day sharpshooting with the enemy. If you stuck your head above the breastworks a minute, a dozen balls would penetrate it and we lost several men, killed and wounded, in the regiment. We had no shelter from the sun, rolling in the clay of the ditches; we were as dirty as hogs, and awfully lousy.

Oh ye patters of nicety, Oh ye Broadway Dandies, Oh ye Brussels Carpet Patriots, what do ye think of this? Think of a great big louse, preying with greedy touch on your fastidious limbs, - think of this and ask yourselves if you could be a soldier and abandon your band-box proclivities for love of country.

We stayed in these works now 17 days without relief, worn out, tired, dirty and sleepy. During this time we had one false alarm, and a great deal of useless firing and nothing else of importance, tho' we were kept constantly on the lookout for mortar shells which were dropped among us every now and then, sometimes killing and wounding several. During this time we had F . Moore wounded in the arm, J. J. Clark killed by a sharpshooter, and J. J. Garoin wounded dangerously in the mouth. We were then relieved for two days, but are now in the works again, when I write this, July 14, 1864.

July 15th. All quiet along the lines except continual sharpshooting and mortar shelling. Nobody hurt in the Regiment. Early in Maryland created a great disturbance in Yankeedom. Awful hot and dusty in the ditches.

July 16th. Nothing unusual. Sharpshooting still going on. One man of Company D killed by sharpshooters, Wm. Ritchey. No one else hurt. Rumors are rife, but nothing reliable. See no prospects of relief. Rations very scarce, and men all anxious for a change.

July 17th. React again the monotonous scenes of yesterday. Another man of Company D killed, Joe Armstrong. It is Sunday and contrary to their usual mode of acting, the Yankees are rather quiet, only threw a few mortar shells in the ditches.

July 18th. A mortar shell fell in the ditches this morning causing some tall skeedadling, but fortunately did not burst. Very anxious to hear from Early in Yankeedom. Cannot hear a word of news. Another man wounded in the regiment this morning. The Yankees keep balls continually flying over our heads, and no man can expose his head a minute above the breastworks without being struck, and most probably killed.

We have had no rain in two months, and the dust is stifling. Living on corn bread and bacon, with cow peas occasionally. Will not be apt to get anything better this summer. Here is General D. H. Hill just passing by inspecting the works, a stern looking old warrior in full uniform. Brigadiers and Colonels are as thick as blackberries and hardly arouse attention, they are so common.

July 19th. Today a change long looked for, but very unpleasant, to the weather worn soldier, took place. The clouds were overspread by a gloomy pall, the atmosphere became dull and sultry, and at length the flood gates of Heaven were opened, and rain, rain, descended in torrents, as if venting its long pent up rage on our devoted heads. Blankets, tent clothes, oil cloths &c. were greatly in demand, and everyone was busy amid the pelting storm fixing up a shelter. But the wetting was the least of our inconveniences. Remember, we are in ditches of red clay, and as the rain mixed with the sticky clay, mud became the consequence.

It rained all day and by evening the mud was actually in places knee deep, and if we moved at all we were compelled to walk in mud ankle deep every step. It was truly an inviting prospect, (knowing that if the mud became waist deep we would have to stay here.) Imagine our appearance, clad in all the beauty of our clay colored habitats, sheltering under the kindly protection of a diminutive oil-doth from the pelting rain, and standing with stoic composure knee deep in mud and water, but it is all "Pur Palaria", and you would be surprised to hear peals of laughter at the unfortunate fall of some clumsy individual, and the jokes cracked with all the jovial mirth of better days.

Gradually the rain ceased and the men, ever ready for improvement, began to remove the muddy clay until he came to more stable ground. Thus we passed the day. Nothing occurred to excite attention, and the night closed in all quiet. Early is now safe out of Maryland after having frightened old Abe to death, captured an immense amount of plunder, horses, cattle &c. whipped the enemy in a pitched battle at Monocacy, and accomplished the greatest raid on record. I was in hopes his designs were against Washington or Baltimore, but it seemed not. Grant is still in our front and keeps up a liberal display of men and wagons. The enemy throw a few more shells but to no effect. Nobody hurt in the Regiment today. Received a letter from home today with some much needed funds, $150.00.

July 20th. A few mortar shells were thrown into our lines this morning but no harm done. The usual sharpshooting going on. It is feared the enemy are tunneling under our lines, and as right in our front is the most favorable spot for such works and as a battery is also here, we are preparing for such a device by digging a tunnel all along the whole face of the battery to meet their's if they have any. Not quite so muddy today, but warm and sultry.

July 21st. Today I got leave to visit the city of Petersburg and found it a great luxury to get in the rear for a short time to clean up and get a good dinner. Nothing new occurred in the trenches today.

July 22nd. Very warm. and sunny. The enemy threw a good many mortar shells at us this morning but hurt no one. Sharpshooters still at work.

July 23rd. Last night we were relieved to rest for a day or two and retired about one mile in rear of the works. Today I am on guard so I get but little rest. Good news from Georgia. Sherman thoroughly whipped by Hood.

July 25th. All quiet. Go back to the ditches tonight." (His last entry.)

EPILOGUE

"Samuel Catawba Lowry was killed July 30th, 1864 at Petersburg, Va. during the Battle of the Crater. The engagement that followed the explosion lasted all day and Sam fell four or five hours after the mine was sprung while leading and spurring his men on to action. He was acting Captain, his higher officers having been either killed or wounded at the time. Thus, at the tender age of nineteen and one half years, with that lofty courage and absolute absence of fear and disregard of self, he laid down his life for his beloved south and for the cause he had defended with such devotion and loyalty.

His diary is a continuous record of his war experiences up to five days before his death. It is a marvel of literary style for so young a boy, and how it was kept at all under the hardships of the camp life, constant shifting back and forth on long marches, thru skirmishes and battles down in the ditches, and above all, that it should have been rescued after the battle and brought back with his remains, is a wonder almost incredible, - if the diary itself did not testify to its truth.

The poems, essays, &c. attached were written by him during the period of war and are evidences of a versatile and splendid mentality, a budding genius, whom, if he had been spared, would have illumined the fields of literature and poetry.

His faithful servant, Henry Avery, a young negro boy, found his body after the battle and performed the almost miraculous feat (in those days of slow transit and general confusion) of getting thru the lines and bringing his master's remains back to his old home in Yorkville, S. C. where he was buried from the Episcopal Church in the family burying ground.

On the day that Sam's body arrived the family was accompanied to the depot by a beautiful dog named Major that had belonged to and been a beloved pet of his. The dog seemed to sense the tragedy and showed every evidence of grief and understanding. The next morning the dog was found dead before the door of the room where his master's body had lain for the night."

/s/ Willie M. Lowry

(Mrs. Sumter L.)

ROLL OF COMPANY, OF WHICH S. CATAWBA LOWRY WAS A MEMBER MAY 7TH, 1864

Capt. J. W. Avery.	
1st Lieut. D. I. Logan,	Killed June 18th
2nd Lieut. W. S. Moore,	Wounded May 20th
Jr. 2nd Guntharp,	
1st Sgt. William Dunovant,	Promoted Capt. Co. C.
2nd Sgt. P. Martin,	Discharged
3rd Sgt. G. W. Moore,	
4th Sgt. W. H. Mitchell,	
5th Sgt. F. Happerfield	Exchanged to H Legion Cavalry
1st Corp. E. J. Downy,	
1st Corp. L. M. Hope,	Died
1st Corp. J.G. Latham.	
1st Corp. S. C. Lowry,	Lieut. Pvt. 2nd
Pvt. A. Behler.	
Pvt. W. T. Behler,	
Pvt. Noah Bias.	
Pvt. E. H. Bridges,	Wounded June 18th
Pvt. F. H. Bridges,	
Pvt. John Caldwell,	
Pvt. J. W. Caldwell,	
Pvt. R. P. Caldwell,	
Pvt. W. M. Caldwell,	

Pvt. Thomas Carroll,
Pvt. W. Carroll,   Exchanged
Pvt. R. L. Caveny,
Pvt. J. L. Clark,
Pvt. J. B. Collins,
Pvt. G. A. Craig,
Pvt. D. A. Currence,
Pvt. M. Derrex,
Pvt. I. W. Dicks,
Pvt. Acy Dover,
Pvt. F. Dover, .
Pvt. D. Dover,
Pvt. J. W. Downy,
Pvt. E. I. Feemster,
Pvt. I. J. Garvin,   Wounded July 10th
Pvt. Jerry Green,
Pvt. W. A. Hays,
Pvt. T. S. Hughes,
Pvt. S. W. Jackson,
Pvt. A. S. Jefferys,
Pvt. J. C. Kirkpatrick,
Pvt. James Martin
Pvt. William Martin,   Killed in battle May 20th
Pvt. B. F. L. Massey   Corp.
Pvt. R. H. Mitchell,
Pvt. Farmer Moore,   Wounded July
Pvt. G. M. Moore,
Pvt. J. W. Moore,
Pvt. G. A. Morehouse,
Pvt. W. V. Moss,
Pvt. W. R. Murphy

Pvt. R. Mulholland,
Pvt. J. L. Parker,
Pvt. R. G. Packer,
Pvt. James Plaxico,
Pvt. J. L. Plaxico ,
Pvt. J. A. Pollard,
Pvt. R. S. Randall,
Pvt. W. L . Randall,
Pvt. R. F. Roberts,
Pvt. Samuel Roberts,
Pvt. Joseph Seapoch,
Pvt. Phil Seapoch,
Pvt. W. E. Sherer,
Pvt. Hugh Sherer,   Wounded
Pvt. R. S. Stewart,
Pvt. J. W. Swezy,   Exchanged
Pvt. T. S. Tippings,   Corp.
Pvt. J. P. Turner,
Pvt. G. W. White,
Pvt. W. R. Whitesides,   Corp.
Pvt. R. J. Withers,
Pvt. J. J. Clark,   Killed July 2nd, 1864
Pvt. N. Seapoch

APPENDIX

PROSE COMPOSITION BY S. CATAWBA LOWRY

CO. "F" 17ᵀᴴ REG'T. S.C.V. CAMP

AT GREEN POND MARCH 6 1864

* *

THE RIGHT OF THE SOUTH TO SECEDE FROM THE NORTH

"In the progress of time one's mind, although it may be unskilled, and untutored, in the various wilds of philosophy or, of a calculating but mysterious philanthropy, naturally embraces, with eagerness, and contemplates with patriotic fervor the all important topic of interest, then agitated by not only politicians and statesmen, but by the public voice at large, the subject I have taken is one of more than ordinary importance. It involves, not the idle strife of demagogues, not the futile threats of foreign tyrants, but it involves the fate, the inevitable fate, of a Nation. Yes, it is a National question. The time honored halls of Congress not only re-echoes the furious debate, but the balmy Southern air grows hot with exciting discussion. It is strange that such should be the case when the fate of eight millions of whites depends on its decision. No, - Humanity answers NO. It is now scarce a century since the thirteen original States of the Union thought of casting their lot in one common vessel, of enlisting under one common flag, in view of establishing one common Government. Let us review the process of organization. The thirteen colonial states did not unanimously nor entirely consent to a federation alliance, and it required all the energy and eloquence of such men as Washington, Franklin, Hancock and others to decide the equivocal colonies, but the bend of union finally was sealed.

But was this alliance unconditional? Was this a Monarchial or hereditary alliance? Was this a Universal, homogeneous compact, or was it not the will, the accepted agreement of independent Sovereign States? Let him who has read and understood the fundamental constitution, formed by our virtuous progenitors answer this. If I understand aright that compact, that union of power, destroyed not the right of State Sovereignty; it did not inculcate as necessary the destruction of State Governments, State Laws, State Boundaries, &c. but only required a mutual support, a mutual contribution, from those several States to support the common Government. Of course, this common government was supreme, as long as justice and equality were equally distributed. It provided for the National defense, the National Subsistence, and was bound to protect the National and State rights from imposition and injustice. It had a fundamental constitution to go by, and beyond that was forbidden ground. It is useless for me to go through the minute details of the constitution; it is too well understood and has been expounded to the entire satisfaction of the public by wiser heads than mine, and the point I wish to prove, the Right of State Sovereignty, has been universally admitted.

The next point is, how far does that right extend, and what is that right? The right of State Sovereignty is a right legitimately decreed by a judicial assembly of legislators. It is a right internally powerful within the State as far as it does not come in antagonism with the constitution of the common government. It is a right internally valid, but externally now. It is a kind of sub jurisdiction subdivided to the common government, only as far as the established constitution, and pressing National necessity required. It is a right formed by the free will of the people, with a knowing sanction of the constitution, and consequently legal. Moreover, it is a right universally recognized by foreign governments, and until now undisputed by our "precocious" brethren; otherwise, why are we called the United States of America? Why are we defined by the most ardent partisans of unity, not as a "League of undisputed Sovereignties." Why did our noble forefathers reject with haughty disdain the "Symbol of Nationality," by refusing a National name? Why were not Sate boundaries, State Laws, State Governments, abolished? And we emerged in one common State? With the same institutions, the same laws as England or France, and we became from the frigid lakes and ice clad hills of Labrador to the tropical Gulf of Mexico, one Homogeneous Republic, Empire or Kingdom, as the people might desire.

These and a host of other well founded reasons might be given in support of any argument. Knowing then these reasons, is it any longer doubtful on which side is right? Has not the south then by the simple right of Sate Sovereignty a perfect undisputable right to secede from the Union? When its dearest privileges, its sacred functions, are compromised? When its total aggrandizement is sought for as a means of remuneration to the North. Where an abolition congress by means of a "Majority of Votes" can pass laws and enact proclamations detrimental to the interest, welfare and safety of the south? Where the emancipation of slaves and destruction of African bondage is one of their principal aims? And when the debasement of their more noble southern brothers is most ardently desired. These inevitable and (by the Yankees) expressed consequences loom up before our view like a blackening cloud dimmed in the distance, but gradually assuming proportions awful in their magnitude until skepticism itself has ceased to wonder and man is appalled by the warded calamity for a season, but rouses from his apathy and binds every energy toward off the fatal result. Is the so called rebellion of the south then any longer a wonder?

Is it in the law of nature to submit to unjust oppression? No, - the vilest reptile that crawls the earth scorns such indignities. WE, We must rise, - must rise and drive back the tide of oppression, or be swept with irresistible force to an ocean of misery or dwell forever in a hateful servitude buried beneath the stormy billows of a joyless inglorious oblivion. The past will be no longer remembered and these scenes of terrestrial bliss, of unalloyed freedom, or glorious deeds, will either be baptized with the oblivious waters of Lethe, or remain forever as puzzling a problem as the "Marble Hieroglyphics in the Halls of Carnah". But before proceeding farther in this strain allow me to bring forward another and conclusive argument to the people. Now, some of these States see that justice is not equally distributed to them with their brother States. They imagine that wrong has been done them and they are not disposed to submit to injustice and resolve to break an alliance fraught with injury to their interest and welfare by renouncing the benefits as well as the dangers of the former union and falling back on their Sate Sovereignty, establish entirely an independent Government. The remaining States forbid this oblivious right and endeavor by force of arms to restore a union formed by the free will of the people. They raise Navies, levy troops, and hire mercenaries to endeavor to accomplish by "Vis Armee" what they cannot, "Lex Talionis". Is it not plain on which side right is? Can you any longer doubt the legality as well as justice of the south's proceedings?

In Republics it has been said, with truth, that it is the "Vox Populi" that rules, not the "Vox Pegi", and from this the doctrine that minorities should acquiesce to only one common government and one common state. But can it hold true in a league of several smaller republics joined together by common consent for common protection? Should the northern states be allowed to carry everything before them because they have the majority of voters? If so, they could vote out the existence of the south; they could destroy every southern institution, and at last as a "magnificent finale" assume the entire reins of a government? This would be serving the seeds of a most tyrannical oligarchy. It would be a stepping stone to tyranny by the means of which every remaining particle of former freedom would be erased, and we would remain the foot-stool of northern malignity.

Enough then has been said to establish my point. Necessity itself compels our proceeding and now the Rubicon has been crossed. The die is cast; and an impossible barrier intervenes between the once friendly brethren. For three years now the struggle between Northern fanaticism and Southern spirit has been going on. On the part of the north it is war of aggression, a war of oppression, and a war for possession, but the south it is a struggle for freedom for all that is dear to the heart for our homes; our altars and firesides; and very existence itself. The vandal foe is the hireling invader and prosecutes with a mercenary spirit, a war of injustice and debasement. From the steep banks of the Potomac to the far flowing Rio Grande; for the marshy swamps of Florida to the grass covered plains of Missouri; from east to west; from north to south; the hated foe encircle us; the roar of hostile cannon is born far on the still night breeze and rouses the fierce ire; the determined courage of every native southerner; every battlefield has proved but too truly to the enemy the invincible spirit of resistance and has fairly demonstrated that equivocal question that Southern courage can meet with success; northern duplicity and treachery. The battles fought on the soil of the old Dominion as well as those fought in other states prove but too truly this fact. Is there then a cause to despair? Are we not as resolute as at the beginning? Have we not proved our ability to defend our rights on may a well contested battleground? And what we have done, can we not do over?

Let every man do his duty and warrant me, all will be well. It is not sufficient that the soldier alone should do his duty, no – the farmers, the exempts, the manufacturers, all must add his might to the common subsistence. Let the cadaverous speculator be abolished. Let him be hooted at as the destroyer of his country; let the skulker be forced from his hiding hole and compelled to do at least a servile duty; let the deserter meet his just reward at the end of a hempen tether, and mark, the effect will be electrical. It will encourage those nobly striving to do their duty in the field to increased exertions and resuscitate at least the vital spark of freedom. Look back thru the dark vista of past ages and review the history of republics and nations.

Has it ever been known that a Nation numbering as many men, possessing as wide an extent of territory, and fighting for as just a cause as the south has to be subjugated? No. Such never has, nor never will be, before us in at least a hateful light; true, the enemy have succeeded in overrunning part of our territory, but is that a cause of despair? No. It should only be a new part of our territory, but is that a cause of despair? No. It should only be a new stimulant to our efforts, and should nerve our arms to strike with redoubled energy every blow for freedom. Our forefathers did not despair when overrun by Britain's troops, but increased their efforts until an all wise God crowned their arms with deserved success. Have we then so degenerated in spirit, in courage, in perseverance, as to despair at such prospects? Has the blood of our ancestors become so extinct in our veins? No. God prevent it. We can at least imitate their example and make a concerted, a glorious stroke for freedom and the unflinching will of a just Providence will award success to the righteous cause. S. C. Lowry, Co. F, 17th S.C.V."

EULOGY ON GENERAL STONEWALL JACKSON, S.C.V.

"Death who knocks with an equal hand at the cottage door and the palace gate has been busy at her appointed work. Morning prevails throughout the land, weeping and wailing testify the fall of the lamented dead." A shadow of gloom rests on every countenance. The whole land is enwrapped in a mantle of grief and sorrow. And for whom? Go ask the soldier lamenting for his commander; go ask the country mourning her favored son; and mark the answer, - "A hero has fallen." The friend of the people, the protector of liberty, and the hero of chivalry has ceased to live. Freedom shrieks louder than she did at Koskinko's fall, for the defeated dead. "The young eagle of the Confederacy, yet unfledged, who so often soared aloft, bearing victory in his talons, has at last yielded to the grim grip of death."

That noble ship whose pennant so often streamed above the battle's roar, and the tempest raged, has at last gone down beneath the still and quiet waters. Well, Oh Death, mayest thou exalt in victory. Well, mayest thou claim the victim, for never have your icy fingers seized a nobler prey; never before has thou caused such universal gloom to be spread on a land. We lament for Jackson; we grieve for the Southern hero; we lament for him who so often led our armies to victory and glory. The great, the good, the benevolent, - he became the adopted son of Liberty and competition fled from him as from a glance of destiny. He, like Napoleon, "Knew no motto but success, he acknowledged no alternative but freedom; he worshipped at no shrine but that of the all powerful, all merciful Creator."

He acknowledged no devotion but his country and his God, and like a true-hearted Christian, gloried in his creed. Need I give an account of his exploits? Are they not familiar to every Southerner; are they not recorded in indelible characters on the glowing shrine of fame and consecrated in memories, fondest recollections? Ay sirs, it is needless. His memories, fondest recollections? Ay sires, it is needless. His exploits are stamped deep into the heart of every Southerner and need no commendation to increase their glory.

He stands on an unapproached eminence, distinguished almost beyond humanity for deliberate courage, cool self-control, remarkable foresight, grand ingenuity, in fine, all the requisites of a great general and a true patriot. The "Public Career of this distinguished Patriot may be described as one triumphant march thru life, neither faltering nor stumbling in ascending to the place of his ambition." "Although not an orator, he could command an influence that mere oratory never wielded. He knew how to inspire his men with confidence in himself and trust in his judgment. He added to the aid of a sound judgment the wisdom of deep calculation and decisive forethought. He was that fiery comet shooting wildly through the realms of space, ravaging with fire and sword the ranks of an oppressing enemy. He was that firm rock against which the waves of a turbulent sea rush in vain, striving to demolish. Peaceful in his disposition, kind to his friends, affectionate to his family, forgiving to his enemies, he conciliated the regard of both good and bad, and wore with equal grade the conquerors wreath and the citizen's gown." "At a time when the Sun of Liberty had nearly set in the gloom of an eternal night beneath the Western horizon, when the noble land was overspread with anxiety and doubt, Jackson arose, and with the magic sway so peculiar to great men --------(illegible) --------------------------country--------------(illegible)------------- enemy through the romantic valleys of Virginia. Behold him and his time worn warriors as they mount the rugged steep and cloud capped mountains. Behold him as he rushed with undaunted bravery upon the very ramparts of tyranny and snatches victory from the hand of a rejoicing conqueror and then, - then see the value of the lamented dead. He is gone, but we trust to reap Celestial rewards for his earthly deeds. "Peace be to his ashes. Calm and quiet may they rest on some vine-clad hill of his own beloved Virginia and let no cunning statue, no marble slab, deface with its mock dignity the Patriot's grave, but rather let the unpruned vine, the uncaged bird, all that speaks of freedom and happiness, decorate a hero's tomb. He needs no monument, no glittering mausoleum, to perpetuate his fame. His name is engraved on the hearts of men, his fame on the pages of history." Composed by S. Catawba Lowry.

"ARE WE REBELS?"

No, - We deny the statement. It is a slander as false as the foul originators themselves. The statistics of our history, the records of the past, and the untrammeled spirit of our people all disavow and hurl back the foul calumniation to its unprincipled instigators. One would think that I am, as some are, inveterate opposers of rebellion in and on every occasion. Far from it. No, - I am an advocate scepter, when kingdoms, empires and republics are deprived of their just rights by an unjust execution of supreme authority, then it is time for an intelligent and independent people to usurp the rights justly their own. It is in the law of human nature, Ay, - even of nature in its most degraded condition, to submit to unjust persecution. The vilest reptile that crawls the earth abhors the idea. Human nature revolts at such degradation. Degradation that grows with a Nation's prosperity and remains an illegitimate curse to posterity. William Wallace, Scotland's immortal hero, rebelled not without a just cause, but because a tyrant usurped his native rights. Charles II of England vindicated his country's honor and obtained his lawful diadem by a just and successful rebellion. Tiber's patriotic Brutus yielded up his life in just and well founded rebellion while Rome's heroic gladiator came near snatching the unmerciful hero from his glittering throne by a just rebellion. History abounds with numerous instances of well warranted rebellion, but, on the other hand there are instances on the contrary side where a nation or a concourse of people were incited to rebellion by the cunning speech or ambitious individuals or by fancied ill treatment and numerous other causes. These are unlawful, unjust, inhuman rebellions and are sure to end in an ignominious downfall. But enough of this."

S. Catawba Lowry

The March
By S. C. L.

1ST VERSE

The weary soldier plods his way

Along the dusty road

And thinks of those so far away

In lands of east abroad.

2ND VERSE

He thinks of that sequestered spot

Where once in peace he played

The shady grove, the lovely cot

Where Nature's debt he paid.

3RD VERSE

And fondly recalls these scenes of bliss

That blest his infant years

When soothed by mother's loving kiss

He buried all his fears.

A CONFEDERATE SOLDIER'S ELOQUENT WAR

4TH VERSE

But time goes on, and troubles come

His years are full and free

And he has left that pleasant home

To fight for Liberty.

5TH VERSE

Oft beneath the sultry sun

Of some autumnal day

He toiled along with belt and gun

And thought how long the way.

6TH VERSE

Oft again, with quivering steps

He totters on his path

But sternly forward, still he creeps,

Indignant with his wrath.

7TH VERSE

No marshal strains awake the wood

No music goes ahead.

Nothing but the Captain's word

And the soldier's steady tread.

8TH VERSE

But hopeful still they struggle on

Determined to be free

Or reveal the Hero Marmion

And die for Liberty

CLEON.

POLAND
– By S. C. LOWRY

On Vestula's banks a mournful sound

Is borne on the still night breeze

And the Warrior Pole, leaps up with a bound

To battle stern fate's decrees.

He sees the Russian Vandal host

In glittering line deploy

He grasps his blade, and stands his post

Determined to destroy.

Revenge ! – Fierce, fearful grows his face

And eager he seeks his foe,

The invader, the Scourge of his race

In increasing numbers grow.

Is it with weak and feeble cry

He shouts the battle charge?

No ! His shout is the beacon of victory

Or death's sad mournful dirge.

Oh Poland ! My Country, My all,

Is this thy mournful doom,

Must we before a Russian fall

And beg a Russian boon?

Yon silvery heights, once proud and fair

In grandeur truly grand

Must they too, with foul despair

Bedeck a vanquished land?

Yon pearly stream once slowly rolled

Its whispering, joyful tide,

But now, Alas ! By foes patrolled,

Oh! What does this betide?

The gloomy Baltic once stretched forth

To grasp Vistula's banks

From East to West, from South to North

Enclosed her Marshalled ranks.

Koskinsko once graced this land

And the great Sobuska's race

Can it be that now she stands

Overwhelmed with disgrace?

But reader stop! Before you place

That lasting signal seal,

Consider first this foul disgrace

Was wrought by Russian steel.

The bonfire blaze, The reeking walls

Bespeak the Russian Foe

Yet Poland stands and grimly calls

Defiance to his foes.

Defiant may she ever be

May victory be her lot,

But death to all eternity

Be Russia's fatal lot

Oh, thou the God of War preside,

And guard the Polish Spears

And grant that peace may yet betide

To drown her suffering tears.

                                        Bonega.

A CONFEDERATE SOLDIER'S ELOQUENT WAR

POETRY BY S. C. L.

ON OUR GENERALS

Ye Southrons look up and see
    Your glittering phalanx stand
Its ranks are thin, but stern and free
    As any Marshalled band.
In front is our noble Lee
    And valorous Beauregard,
The one the soul of Liberty
    The other our safe guard.
And there is cautious Bragg too,
    And Longstreet, bold and free
With Ewell ever firm and true
    Defenders of the Free
Lo! Johnston stands amid the first
    With Hood and A. P. Hill
Who are, by every Yankee curse
    For the sake of Gaine's Mill.
We have not finished with them all,
    For there's Smith's to double twice

And Major General John McCall

    To mate with Sterling Price.

Dick Taylor yet remains there still

    And Breckenridge in turn,

Besides General D. H. Hill

    And fighting Pat Clayburne,

Our country looks with candor on

    With unimpassioned eyes

At Polk, Stuart and VanDorn

And Virginia's noble wises

    There is Hampton yet to name

And Loring Buckner Hall,

    Who rank high on the roll of fame

May they never fall.

    The chivalrous Morgan with his troop

Has received a mead of praise

    And Forrest, Wheeler, Whorton too

Are sung in minstrels lays.

    Our cause is yet upheld

By Pickett, Kemper, Lee,

    With Jenkins yet to weld

The bond of Liberty.

    There is Early and the gallant Law

With Evans immortal few,

    Hindman, French come up to Law

And show your vigor too.

    Walker still, and Marmaduke

Are amid the favored few

    With Magruder to rebuke

The Yankee hirling crew.

My list is full but others still

    Deserve a Nation's thanks,

Tho by my memory forgotten

    Is our Army's Marshaled ranks,

The private soldier above all

    Deserves a Country's praise;

Their fame will stand and never fall

    Until eternity decays.

        By – S. Catawba Lowry

A CONFEDERATE SOLDIER'S ELOQUENT WAR

MAGGIE BY MY SIDE – A SONG

1ST VERSE

The land of my home is flitting, flitting from my view,

A sail in the gale is sitting, toils the merry crew.

Here let my home be on the waters wide,

I'll roam with a proud heart, Maggie's by my side.

CHORUS

My own loved Maggie dear,

Sitting by my side

Maggie dear, my own love

Sitting by my side

2ND VERSE

The wind howling o'er the billow, from the distant lea

The storm raging around my pillow, brings no care to me,

Roll on ye dark waves o'er the troubled tide,

I need not your anger, Maggie's by my side.

3ᴿᴰ VERSE

Storms can appall me never while her brow is clear

Fair weather lingers ever where her smiles appear

When sorrow's breakers around my heart shall hide

Still may I find her sitting by my side.

S. Catawba Lowry

Made in the USA
Charleston, SC
25 May 2010